Devotional Songs of

NARSĪ MEHTĀ

PLATE I. Narsi Mehtā and his bhajan-singing companions. Stone images at Gopnath Temple near Talaja; date unknown.

Devotional Songs of
NARSĪ MEHTĀ

Translated by
SWAMI MAHADEVANANDA

With an introduction by
SIVAPRIYANANDA

MOTILAL BANARSIDASS PUBLISHERS
PRIVATE LIMITED • DELHI

First Published: 1985
Reprint: Delhi, 1995

ISBN: 81-208-0509-7

Also available at:

MOTILAL BANARSIDASS

41 U.A. Bungalow Road, Jawahar Nagar, Delhi 110 007
120 Royapettah High Road, Mylapore, Madras 600 004
16 St. Mark's Road, Bangalore 560 001
Ashok Rajpath, Patna 800 004
Chowk, Varanasi 221 001

PRINTED IN INDIA

BY JAINENDRA PRAKASH JAIN AT SHRI JAINENDRA PRESS,
A-45 NARAINA, PHASE I, NEW DELHI 110 028
AND PUBLISHED BY NARENDRA PRAKASH JAIN FOR
MOTILAL BANARSIDASS PUBLISHERS PRIVATE LIMITED,
BUNGALOW ROAD, DELHI 110 007

CONTENTS

Introduction
1

Translator's Note
21

ŚṚṄGĀRA NĀ PADO [1—40]
23

ŚṚṄGĀRA MĀLĀ [41—70]
67

BHAKTI, JÑĀNA ANE
VAIRĀGYA NĀ PADO [71-100]
103

Bibliography
141

Index
143

LIST OF PLATES

Frontispiece

Narsī Mehtā and his bhajan-singing companions. Stone images at Gopnath Temple near Talaja; date unknown.

Between pages 16 *and* 17

1. Narsī Mehtā's school; a cell in the second century A.D. Buddhist caves near Talaja, Bhavnagar.
2. The Gopnath Temple near Talaja.
3. The Dāmodara Temple and Tank (sixteenth century A.D.) at the foot of Girnar hills, Junagadh.
4. Śrī Nāthjī—Lord of Śrī (Lakṣmī)—Aspect of Kṛṣṇa worshipped at Nathdwara (Rajasthan), the principal seat of the Vallabhācārya sect. In this image, Kṛṣṇa stands with his left hand raised to hold mount Govardhana (after a pichvāī painting).
5. The rāsa-dance (after a coloured lithoprint published by S.S. Brijbasi and Sons, Mathura, U.P.)
6. A Nathdwara pichvāī showing the rāsa-dance.
7. Veṇugopāla—Mysore style painting, late nineteenth century A.D.

A NOTE ON THE TRANSLITERATION OF INDIAN WORDS

In transcribing the various Sanskrit and Gujarati words, the current convention of diacritical marks is used. Only geographical names are given without the diacritical marks, e.g. Junagadh instead of Junāgaḍh and Vrindavana instead of Vṛndāvana, as such words are now in common use and do not need diacritical marks to denote their correct pronunciation.

Om Gajānanāya namaḥ

INTRODUCTION

Narsī Mehtā was born at a time when Muslim rule had been firmly established in Gujarat. In A.D. 1411, Ahmedabad had become the capital of Ahmed Shah I, the third Sultan of Gujarat. Frequent Muslim raids into Saurashtra had disturbed its social and political stability. Traditional Hindu society was being shaken at its very roots. In literature, the influence of Sanskrit court poetry had almost disappeared. Even Jainism, which had been the main creative force in the literature of Gujarat for more than five centuries, was fighting a losing battle for survival against the new folk literature which was becoming very popular under the influence of the cult of bhakti.

The word 'bhakti' comes from the Sanskrit root *bhaj* which means 'to serve', 'to adore' and 'to honour'. In the religious sense it refers to the doctrine of adoration for a personalized God (iṣṭadevatā). The idea of bhakti was not new to Hinduism. It was mentioned in the *Śvetāśvatara Upaniṣad* (c. 500 B.C.) and later very clearly expounded in the *Bhagavad-gītā* (c. 300 B.C.) by Kṛṣṇa himself. The most complete glorification of the bhakti doctrine was given in the *Bhāgavata Purāṇa* (between A.D. 500 and A.D. 900), a text which is still considered to be the greatest single sourcebook of bhakti and the mythology of Kṛṣṇa.

The philosophical nature of bhakti was defined by Nārada and Śāṇḍilya (both c. A.D. 900) in their respective *Bhaktisūtras* as 'supreme love for God'. Many later scholars and philosophers built entire systems of philosophy on the simple, basic idea of intense devotion to a personalized God. The most important of these philosophers, whose sects still survive and have a large following, were: Rāmānuja (born A.D. 1027), Nimbārka (born A.D. 1130), Madhva (born A.D. 1197), Viṣṇusvāmin (fourteenth century A.D.) and his follower Vallabhācārya (A.D. 1478-1530).

The medieval revival of the path of bhakti was, however, only indirectly based on the works of the great scholars and philosophers. Its real inspiration came from the strongly emotional hymns, of very great literary merit, composed in the language of the people by early Tamil saints: the Vaiṣṇava Āḷvārs and the Śaiva Nāyaṇārs (from A.D. 300-800). By the thirteenth century A.D., the cult of bhakti and the tradition of composing emotionally charged devotional songs in the spoken languages spread from the Tamil-speaking areas to Karnataka and Maharashtra. A Sanskrit verse that is often quoted in the early Purāṇas says:

> Bhakti was born in the Draviḍa country, developed and flourished in Karnataka, had some success in Maharashtra, but disappeared when it reached Gujarat.

The most important feature of the bhakti cult was the great stress it laid on sincere and intense devotion to a personal, all-loving and gracious God. The purity of personal character was stressed instead of caste status, and empty rites and ceremonials were worthless when compared to a loving heart. All caste distinctions were abandoned, and the path of bhakti was open to the high-born Brahmins as well as to the lowest of the untouchables. Quite a number of the bhaktas were actually members of the lower castes of Hindu society.

The bhaktas preached that there was no need to use the complicated philosophical process of reasoning in order to understand the divine. Deep love of God, the constant repetition of his names, and the steady company of other devotees was enough to bring God's grace and to reach everlasting union with the divine.

Though orthodox ceremonials were shunned, nine well-defined aids to bhakti were recongnized. These helped the devotee to establish a personal and intimate relationship with the desired form of the deity. The nine are, according to the *Bhāgavata Purāṇa* (VII, 5, 23): hearing (śravaṇa) and singing (kīrtana) the praise of the Lord; remembering (smaraṇa) his names at all times; serving (pādasevana), worshipping (arcana) and bowing low (vandana) to his lotus feet; complete servitude (dāsya), a strong and intimate relationship (sakhya) and absolute surrender (ātma-nivedana) to the Lord.

There were never any restrictions regarding the deity to which a bhakta's devotion was to be directed. A strong, sincere, and steadfast devotion to any deity, or for that matter even to the formless Brahman of the *Upaniṣads*, could bring about the same spiritual results. But in spite of this rather catholic freedom to devote oneself to any deity, most medieval saint-poets dedicated themselves to the two most popular incarnations of Viṣṇu in the form of Rāma and Kṛṣṇa: Rāma as the embodiment of righteousness and absolute truth; and Kṛṣṇa as the personification of love and the divine joy that destroys all pain.

The emotion of bhakti (bhakti-bhāva) can take many forms, depending upon the psychological nature of the devotee. The bhakta may take the emotional attitude of a servant to his master (dāsya); or of one friend to another (sakhya); or of a parent to a child (Vātsalya); or of a child to a parent (śānta); or of a wife to her husband (kānta); or of a beloved to her lover (rati or mādhurya); or of a god-hater towards god (dveśa). In fact, it did not matter in the least what the individual's emotional feeling was towards god, as long as there was an overpowering, unshakable, emotional intimacy. Rāvaṇa, the evil king of Lanka in the *Rāmāyaṇa* epic, hated Rāma so much that he constantly remembered him. Through his hatred he attained salvation.

Another chief distinguishing feature of the medieval bhakti mārga was that almost all its exponents composed and recited songs and poems, full of the most fervent devotion, in the language of the people. They discarded the use of the traditionally sanctified religious language Sanskrit, so that more and more people could understand the basic doctrine of devotion to a personal, living, humane God; and this led to the rapid and widespread popularity of the cult of bhakti.

Narsī Mehtā

The greatest, and perhaps the most significant bhakta-poet of Gujarat was Narsī Mehtā. He belonged to the very rigidly orthodox and prosperous caste of Nāgar Brahmins of Vagnagar (near Mehsana in north Gujarat). Unlike the life of many medieval bhakta-poets, the life-events of Narsī Mehtā are well recorded. Though later accounts have added many legends and tales describing miracles, the basic facts of his biography are quite easy to reconstruct.

The poet himself has left us three complete autobiographical works: *Śāmaḷśā no vivāh* (marriage of son Śāmaḷśā), *Kunvarbāi nu māmerun* (incidents relating to the gifts given by Narsī Mehtā to his daughter Kunvarbāi in the seventh month of her first pregnancy), and *Hār-mālā* (garland incident). Besides these three works, there are numerous verses on isolated events in his life. Many later Gujarati poets, in particular Viśvanāth Jāni (c. A.D. 1652) and Premānand (A.D. 1636-1734), have written long poems describing the life of Narsī.[1] By the seventeenth century A.D., primarily on account of Jāni's works, Narsī Mehtā's fame had spread well beyond the borders of Gujarat to be included in Nābhājī's (A.D. 1634-55) famous *Bhakta māla* (garland of devotees), an account of Vaiṣṇava saints.

Narsī Mehtā's grandfather, Viṣṇudās worked as the head clerk in the court of the devout Vaiṣṇava ruler Rā Muktāsinh (A.D. 1373-97) of Junagadh. After Viṣṇudās' death, Narsī's father Kṛṣṇadās was unemployed for a long time and so returned to Talaja, a small town about 30 kilometers south of modern Bhavnagar, where the family probably had an ancestral house. Kṛṣṇadās had had two sons and a daughter before Narsī's birth, but they had all died in childhood.

Narsī was born at Talaja when his father was quite an old man. According to the traditionally accepted date, Narsī was born on the second day of the bright half of the lunar month of Mārgaśīrṣa (November-December) in the Vikrama-samvat (s.) year 1470 (A.D. 1414).[2] Most modern scholars accepts this traditional date. The only scholar to raise any serious doubt was K. M. Munshi, who tried to place Narsī's birth sometime between s. 1530 (A.D. 1474) and s. 1580 (A.D. 1522). His arguments have found very little support.

Kṛṣṇadās died in s. 1473 (A.D. 1417) when Narsī was only three years old. After his father's death, Narsī and his mother Dayākor went to live with Parvatdās, Narsī's paternal uncle. It is not certain as to where Parvatdās actually lived. Tradition says he lived in Talaja; Viśvanāth Jāni says he lived in Junagadh; and Vallabhadās says he lived in Mangrol, a small coastal town south-west of Junagadh.

A popular legend tells us that the child Narsī could not speak. At the age of eight, he started speaking after being blessed by a wandering Vaiṣṇava monk. Some say that this wandering monk was no other than the great south Indian scholar, philosopher and founder of the Rudra sampradāya, Viṣṇusvāmin. There is, however, no historical evidence for this legend.

If we follow the traditional account of Narsī's early life, his childhood was spent in Talaja. He probably went to the local school with his cousins, where he learnt the Gujarati language of his day, and perhaps a little Sanskrit. His religious education was done at home by his mother and uncle Parvatdās who were both devout Vaiṣṇavas. They must have certainly taught him the basic philosophy of their sect and the Viṣṇu-Kṛṣṇa mythology from the *Bhāgavata* and other *Purāṇas*. At the early age of eleven, according to custom, Narsī was engaged to be married to the daughter of a wealthy Nāgar gentleman. But the engagement was broken off when it was discovered that Narsī was no good at studies, and that he spent most of his time either with wandering mendicants or sitting alone in little caves. A small cell in the complex of second century A.D. Buddhist caves in the hill near Talaja is still identified as the 'school' of Narsī Mehtā. Most of Narsī's co-students considered him to be rather odd and abnormal as he frequently dressed himself up in the women's clothes and danced in front of the religious mendicants.

In about s. 1481 (A.D. 1425) Narsī's mother died. His uncle Parvatdās, in order to carry on Narsī's family line and hoping that he would settle down to a more conventional life, married him to a Nāgar girl named Māṇekbāi, the daughter of one Raghunāth Puruṣottam. This was in the year s. 1484 (A.D. 1428). Soon after Narsī's marriage, Parvatdās died[3] and Narsī and his wife went to live in the house of his cousin Bansīdhar. Narsī frequently refers to Bansīdhar as 'bhāi' (brother) and this has led many late biographers to consider him as Narsī's real brother. Premānand says that Bansīdhar was his cousin and this is quite likely.

It is customary in Gujarat to refer to all male first cousins as brothers.

Marriage made no difference to Narsī Mehtā's way of life. He still danced and sang in the company of holy men, and made no attempts to earn money to support his wife. One day Bansīdhar's wife called Narsī a pervert and burden to their family. Narsī was of a very delicate, soft and almost feminine nature. The harsh, and to his innocent mind, undeserved words of his cousin's wife pierced his heart very deeply. He left their house and walked to Gopnath, a small, deserted village on the eastern coast of Saurashtra, and about 40 kilometers from Talaja. In the middle of this deserted village stood an unused Śiva temple. Here, Narsī decided to end his life by starvation. He says:

> The offensive words of my brother and his wife so pained Narsī's heart, that I left home, went to live in the forest, and there served Śiva with all sincerity. On Monday, the 7th day of the bright half of Caitra (March-April), Narsī decided to stay in the forest and perform severe penance unto death.

For seven days, from the 7th to the 14th of the month of Caitra, s. 1484 (A.D. 1428), Narsī sat in the temple of Gopnath without water or food. He became weak and delirious. Then suddenly his body trembled, and he went into an ecstatic trance. In this trance state, he saw Śiva appear before his very eyes. Śiva asked him what he wanted. In a song, Narsī describes the incident:

> When Śiva appeared before me, I asked him, 'Oh Lord, I pray you give me a sight of that which is most loved by you.' The great Lord placed upon my head his holy hand, and then I saw, with great delight, the gopīs' dance with the Master of Vaikuṇṭha (Kṛṣṇa).

Narsī Mehtā goes on to tell us that, in the vision, at the request of Rukmiṇī, Kṛṣṇa's wife, he was allowed to hold one of the torches that illuminated the scene. With torch in hand, he watched the most thrilling sight of his life: the rāsa-līlā dance of Kṛṣṇa, as described in the tenth section of the *Bhāgavata Purāṇa*. Kṛṣṇa, Rādhā, the milkmaids of Gokula, and even Kṛṣṇa's wives

Rukmiṇī and Satyabhāmā, danced all night just to please Narsī:

> The beautiful gopī—enjoying the bliss of love play with her Lord,
> A joyful dance, their love enhanced, and Narsī was present there.
> I felt the play of Kṛṣṇa deep in my heart and soul
> And in my life I sing that play, just as my eyes beheld.
> In my hand I held the torch, to light the joyful play
> I sang with rapture at that dance of Gokula's Lord at play.

Narsī Mehtā lost all outer consciousness, the hairs of his body stood on end, he trembled, and his eyes filled with tears of joy. The torch he held burnt his hand. But, like Bernadette, the visionary of Lourdes—who held 'the flaming end of a candle in her hand for fifteen minutes during one of her ecstasies' (Underhill, *Mysticism*, p. 354)—he felt neither pain nor did his flesh show any sign of burning.

Many later biographers, and especially Munshi, suggest that Narsī was taken either to Dwarika or Vrindavan to see a performance of the 'rāsalīlā' as enacted by a professional group of dancers. But from what Narsī says in his own poems, it is likely that the experience was a vision that occurred in a state of ecstatic trance.

Soon after the ecstasy which was to change his life, Narsī went back to his wife, but:

> I danced all day and clapped my hands and sang the praise of God
> They heard this quite far away, then devotees all came
> To sing and beat the time with me. My brother and his wife
> Were angered by all this, and said 'Please live away from us';
> So Narsī took his wife and said 'Let us go to Junagadh'.[4]

Narsī settled in Junagadh. But his life had changed. He was no longer interested in worldly life and cared little for social approval. He spent his time singing and dancing as he had always done, but now he did it with complete abandon. The vision of the divine rāsa-līlā was still fresh in his memory and so he composed songs describing the rāsa dance of Rādhā and Kṛṣṇa with feeling and sensitivity. The songs of the *Śṛṅgāra mālā* and *Śṛṅgāra nā pado*—translated here—were composed at about this time, between the years s. 1484 (A.D. 1428) and s. 1490 (A.D. 1434), the year in which his daughter Kunvarbāi was born. Four years later, Māṇekbāi gave birth to a son who was named Śāmaḷdās (servant of the dark-one) after Kṛṣṇa.

For the 13 years between the birth of his daughter and her marriage to the son of Śrīranga Mehtā of Una, in s. 1503 (A.D. 1447) Narsī Mehtā enjoyed an uneventful, and rather peaceful and settled domestic life. He says that during his stay in Junagadh he was free from all financial worries as he was constantly helped by 'God'. The mother of Rā Māṇḍlik (A.D.1451-72), the ruler of Junagadh, was a pious Vaiṣṇava and it is likely that she secretly helped Narsī Mehtā.

In s. 1504 (A.D. 1484) Kunvarbāi became pregnant. In the seventh month of her first pregnancy, it was customary for her parents to perform a ritual during which presents had to be given to all her in-laws. Narsī had nothing to give. So he was humiliated and ridiculed during the ceremony by all his wealthy castemen in Una. In his own poem called *Māmerun* Narsī describes this incident very graphically. We are told how at the end of all the ridicule and humiliation, Lord Kṛṣṇa and his wife Rukmiṇī saved his honour by providing timely help in the form of rich presents and a lot of gold. Kṛṣṇa, in the form of a wealthy merchant, is said to have helped Narsī in getting his son Śāmaḷdās married in s. 1506 (A.D. 1450), and in clearing a bond (huṇḍi).

In s. 1507 (A.D. 1451) Narsī's wife Māṇekbāi died. He was finally freed from all family ties to devote himself entirely to the worship of his beloved Kṛṣṇa. He now had time to reflect upon the past events of his life, and it is likely that a large number of his autobiographical poems were composed at about this time.

In the poem describing the *Māmerun* incident, Narsī tells us that his son died soon after the death of his wife Māṇekbāi. He also tells us about his own mental state at that time.

I had two children, a boy and a girl.
My son was virtuous and my daughter full of understanding.

My son was married in Vadnagar and my daughter Kunvarbāi
in Una.
Then my wife and son died and all my friends were weeping;
But I could feel no sorrow.
We all have to leave this mortal frame one day.

Kunvarbāi was widowed in about s. 1510 (A.D. 1454) and came to live with her father in Junagadh. Narsī was about 40 years old then and had few family ties left. His widowed daughter and daughter-in-law managed his household as best as they could on the presents given by the devotees and Narsī's royal benefactress. Narsī Mehtā danced and sang devotional songs, which he composed, all day and night. His intense devotion was dedicated to Gopāla Kṛṣṇa, the young cowherd Kṛṣṇa of Gokula and Vrindavan.

Like all medieval bhakta-poets, Narsī laid great stress on purity of character, simplicity and sincere devotion rather than on caste status and book learning. All votaries of God were members of one great family. There could be no narrow caste distinctions between true devotees. So Narsī danced and sang in the homes of the highest of the Brahmins, as well as in those of the untouchables. To him they were all the children of Hari (Harijana).[5]

At the foot of the Girnar hills is the holy tank of the Dāmodara
temple.
There Narsī went every day to bathe.
The untouchables were sincere devotees,
They request me, with folded hands,
'Do dance and sing to bring spirituality into our homes'.

Narsī Mehtā was far more popular with the untouchables and the lower castes than he was with the members of his own caste group. The Nāgars were very orthodox, and had always considered themselves to be the highest and the purest caste of Brahmins in Gujarat. They did not approve of Narsī's association with the untouchables. How could they allow a mad and irresponsible member of their caste to dance all night in the homes of the ritually and socially defiling castes? After many unsuccessful attempts at

restraining Narsī Mehtā from his caste-damaging activities, they excommunicated him. Narsī was not at all perturbed.
He says:

> They say I am impure, and they are right.
> I love only those who love Hari.
> I see no difference between one Harijana and another.
> But those who make such narrow divisions
> Will be born again and again,
> They will never be free.

Both Viśvanāth Jāni and Premānand tell us about the many miracles which induced the Nāgars to reinstate Narsī into his former caste; but all these appear to be afterthoughts to white-wash the injustice of their caste ancestors. Narsī quite categorically states: 'Oh God! I never want to be born again in the narrow-minded caste of Nāgars'.

Insulted by Narsī Mehtā's indifference at being excluded from his former caste, and jealous of his popularity among the people, the Nāgars accused him of immorality and hypocrisy. They also requested the ruler of Junagadh to take steps in order to put an end to Narsī's unorthodox activities. Viśvanāth Jāni and Pre-mānand say that the main complaint of the Nāgar castemen was that Narsī induced women to join his kīrtan-singing group, and that even high caste women were lured into dancing in the houses of the untouchables. One legend says that Narsī was called by Rā Māṇḍlik to prove his innocence and justify his religious views. Narsī Mehtā bravely answered all the charges against him, demon-strated his knowledge of the Hindu scriptures, and finally the doors of the palace temple opened miraculously and Kṛṣṇa put a flower garland around Narsī's neck to prove his complete innocence.

A number of legends have grown around the garland incident which took place in the year S. 1512 (A.D. 1456). Jānī, Prem-ānand and other later biographers mention some of these legends, while others have been circulated orally through folk tales and songs. Several of these have been inserted into Narsī Mehtā's own narrative of the event in *Hār-mālā*. It was on account of these later interpolations that K.M. Munshi considered the entire *Hār-mālā* to be the work of another poet and of a much later date.

In his old age, especially after the death of his patroness, the mother of the ruler of Junagadh, Narsī turned his attention inward. Instead of describing the love play of Rādhā and Kṛṣṇa, he began composing songs and poems that were either philosophical or full of the spirit of renunciation and bhakti. Most of the philosophical songs show a mixture of many ideas, and they are certainly not sectarian. In some of the songs, there is a strong influence of Śaṅkara's idea of this world being an illusion (māyā):

> In sleep I see this world full of pleasures,
> But when I awake there is nothing.
> Existance and Soul are one;
> They are like Brahman before Brahman.

In other poems, Narsī seems to favour the early Vaiṣṇava philosophy of Viṣṇusvāmin that all existance is real and forms parts of the Universal aspects of Kṛṣṇa:

> Oh Hari ! this entire Universe is You,
> All forms are Your forms.
> In the body You are the Soul,
> In the sun You are the brightness,
> In space You are the sound
> That we hear in the Vedas.

In some poems Narsī stresses the popular bhakti idea of complete self-surrender (ātma-nivedana). The devotee places himself, and his Soul, in the hands of his deity, trusting in His will and awaiting His grace:

> What point is there in worrying about the world?
> All is in the hands of the great Lord of the universe.
> Our will amounts to nothing,
> Our salvation lies in calling on Him for help.

In A.D. 1467, when Narsī was 53, Sultan Mahmud Shah I—generally known as Mahmud Begḍa (A.D. 1458-1511)—attacked Junagadh. On receiving a very large tribute from the local ruler, he went back to Ahmedabad, only to return again the next year. Such repeated Muslim raids probably induced Narsī to leave Junagadh. According to traditional accounts, he went back to live in the family house of his uncle in Mangrol. Narsī was fortunate in leaving Junagadh when he did, for in A.D. 1473, it was annexed to the Gujarat Sultanate by Mahmud Begḍa and Rā Māṇḍlik embraced Islam to save his life.

The last years of Narsī Mehtā's life were spent at Mangrol where he probably composed his last work, *Govinda gamana.* In this he describes, in very moving language, the final departure of Kṛṣṇa from Gokula and the heartbreaking lament of his beloved gopīs. In the last verse of this poem, Narsī says:

Singing the Lord's praise I have grown old,
And yet I have not even praised one-hundredth of His infinite qualities.
Today, tomorrow, time has passed away;
Now I am old, but still attached to this illusionary world,
But Narsī has vowed to sing His praise,
So even when his skin has wrinkled,
And his hair has turned gray, he writes this poem.

In s. 1536 (A.D. 1480), at the age of 66, Narsī Mehtā's most eventful life ended. It seems that before his death he had been reconciled with the Nāgar Brahmin caste elders who cremated him and probably performed all the after-death rites. The cremation ground in Mangrol, where Narsī's last mortal remains were burnt, is still known as the 'Narsī's smaśāṇ'.

The Works of Narsī Mehtā

The works of Narsī Mehtā can be classified into four well-defined classes: (1) those that are either free translations of, or based on the tenth section (skandha) of the *Bhāgavata Purāṇa*; (2) those that are inspired by Jayadeva's (twelfth century A.D.) *Gita-govinda*; (3) autobiographical poems; and (4) philosophical/bhakti verses.

In the first class belong the following: *Kṛṣṇa janma* (birth of Kṛṣṇa), *Bāl-lilā* (Kṛṣṇa's childhood play), *Nāga daman* (victory over the snake king), *Dāṇ-līlā* (play with gopīs), *Rāsa līlā* (rāsa dance), *Rāsa sahasrapadī* (1000 verses on the rāsa dance), *Sudāmā carit* (life of Kṛṣṇa's friend Sudāmā), *Mān-līlā* (Kṛṣṇa-gopī love quarrels), *Rukmiṇī vivāh* (Kṛṣṇa's marriage to Rukmiṇī), *Govinda gamana* (the departure of Kṛṣṇa) and many stray devotional songs based on the *Bhāgavata* theme.

The work inspired by Jayadeva's *Gīta-govinda* are: *Cāturī chatrīsī* (36 verses on artful Kṛṣṇa), *Cāturī ṣoḍaśī* (16 verses on artful Kṛṣṇa), *Surat sangrām* (battle of love), *Śṛṅgāra mālā* (garland of love songs), *Śṛṅgāra nā pado* (love poems), *Daśāvatāra nā pado* (verses on the ten incarnations of Viṣṇu), and a number of songs on the spring (vasanta) and swing (hiṇḍoḷ) festivals.

Narsī Mehtā's autobiographical poems and verses are: *Māmerun, Śāmaḷśā no vivāh, Hār-mālā* and other sporadic verses.

All of Narsī's philosophical songs were composed in the later part of his life and over a period of about ten years. They were mostly stray poems composed spontaneously when he was in a reflective mood. Recently, these have been collected together and published under the title of *Jñāna ane Bhakti nā pado* (verses of Wisdom and Devotion).[6]

The Translated Songs of Narsī Mehtā

The 100 songs translated here constitute 40 songs of the *Śṛṅgāra nā pado*, 30 verses that form the work called *Śṛṅgāra mālā*,[7] and 30 philosophical/devotional songs. The 70 verses from the two *Śṛṅgāra* collections treat the theme of Rādhā-Kṛṣṇa love play in a manner similar to the *Gīta-govinda*. The philosophical songs are not systematic philosophy at all, but general ideas of renunciation and the impermanence of life. Whenever a philosophical concept is expressed, as in songs 93 (2), 95 (4) and 99, it is usually very general and popular, rather than logical and systematic.

Kṛṣṇa, who forms the central character of the *Śṛngāra* songs, is generally regarded as the eighth incarnation of Viṣṇu, but according to medieval Vaiṣṇavism, he is the second full (pūrṇa) manifestation of Lord Viṣṇu on earth. He is the embodiment of divine love and supreme spiritual joy, and born at the beginning of the age of darkness and strife (kaliyuga) to establish the religion of love and devotion.

Kṛṣṇa was the son of Devakī, sister of the evil king Kaṃsa of Mathura, and Vasudeva, the prince of the lunar clan (candra-vaṃśa) of the Yādavas. The sāge Nārada had predicted that Kaṃsa would meet his end at the hands of Devakī's son. So the evil king decided to keep his sister and brother-in-law captive. He then brutally killed their six sons soon after they were born. The seventh child Balarāma—considered to be the partial manifestation of Viṣṇu or an incarnation of his serpent (Ādi-śeṣa)—escaped death at the hands of Kaṃsa by being miraculously transferred to the womb of Vasudeva's second wife Rohiṇī.

Kṛṣṇa, the Dark One, was born at midnight on the 8th day of the dark half of the lunar month of Śrāvaṇa (July-August). To protect the divine child from his cruel uncle, he was secretly exchanged for the new-born daughter of a rich cowherd called Nanda and his wife Yaśodā, who lived in Vraja, north of Mathura. Kaṃsa, however, soon discovered this deception and ordered the murder of all male children within the district of Mathura. To further protect the child Kṛṣṇa, his foster parents, along with all the inhabitants of his cowherd settlement went to live in Gokula, a pastoral district reasonably away from Kaṃsa's direct reach. Kṛṣṇa and his half brother Balarāma grew up as cowherds. Even as a child, Kṛṣṇa's beauty was so divine that no one could resist falling in love with him. As a boy, Kṛṣṇa learnt to play the flute—pastoral instrument *par excellence*—so well that its magic charmed all the women of Gokula. Kṛṣṇa would play his flute to lure all the women, both married and unmarried, to the woods and groves of Vrinda trees on the banks of the Yamunā river. There, he would sport with them all night. He would dance with them, make love to them, sometimes even desert them in the middle of love play, and occasionally show more love for one of the milkmaids (Rādhā) to make all the others burn with jealousy.

The evil Kaṃsa could not rest until he had destroyed his future killer. So he sent a host of demons (rākṣasas), in various guises, to kill the boy Kṛṣṇa. All the demons were overcome and killed by the divine child. Eventually, when Kṛṣṇa became a young man, he left Gokula and all the loving gopīs to go to the kingdom of Mathura and kill his evil uncle.

In Mathura, Kṛṣṇa killed Kaṃsa, placed the rightful ruler Ugrasena on the throne, and decided to claim his princely inheritance to the Yādava clan. He completely abandoned the gopīs of Vraja, and went to the hermitage of sage Sandīpani to learn statecraft, the science of war, and other subjects befitting a young prince.

Back in Mathura after his education, he discovered that the peace of the kingdom was threatened by repeated attacks of Jarāsandha of Magadha—father-in-law of Kaṃsa—and a foreign king called Kāla Yavana. So he moved the entire kingdom of Mathura to Dwaraka on the north western coast of Saurashtra (Gujarat), not far from the birth place of Narsī Mehtā. In Dwaraka, Kṛṣṇa assumed the role of a king, and it was as a king that he helped his cousins, the five Pāṇḍava princes, during the great battle that is described in the epic *Mahābhārata*.

Historically, Kṛṣṇa, the son of Devakī, is first mentioned in the *Chāndogya Upaniṣad* (700 B.C.). In this work, he is called a scholar, a philosopher and a disciple of a great mystic, Ghora Āngirasa. He again appears in the *Mahābhārata* (c. 400 B.C.) where his personality is far more developed. He is still a mystic and a philosopher who delivers the celebrated *Bhagavad-gitā* to Arjuna in the middle of the battlefield; but he is also a statesman and an authority on war. In this capacity he advises the Pāṇḍava princes on the conduct of the war. In the *Harivaṃśa* (c. A.D. 200)—an appendix to the *Mahābhārata*—and in the early *Purāṇas* (A.D. 400-800) Kṛṣṇa becomes an incarnation of Viṣṇu. By the time of the *Bhāgavata Purāṇa*, Kṛṣṇa, is pre-eminently the cowherd hero. His princely life fades into the background.

In the *Bhāgavata Purāṇa*, Kṛṣṇa sports with the gopīs and arouses them to divine ecstasy. But among all the milkmaids he has a special favourite Ārādhitā. In the *Bhāgavata Purāṇa* this special gopī is not named,[8] but in the *Gita-govinda*, and in all medieval devotional literature, she is called Rādhā.

Rādhā is the wife of a cowherd called 'Ayanaghoṣa'. But she

has very little interest in family life. She lives for Kṛṣṇa and is overcome with grief when separated from him. At the sound of his flute, she leaves her husband and family and runs to the woods to sport with her beloved. No social pressure can stop her. Most bhakta-poets consider Rādhā to be a symbol of intense devotion, and her social situation an allegory of the soul which is tied to the attractions of the world, and yet yearns for union with the divine. But some later poets, particularly the eight Hindi poets of the 'aṣṭachāp' group, felt uncomfortable about the socially scandalous love affair between Rādhā and Kṛṣṇa. And so, following the sectarian doctrine of Vallabhācārya and his followers, they attempted to make Rādhā a legal consort of Kṛṣṇa by celebrating their wedding just before the latter's departure for Mathura.

In the songs of Narsī Mehtā that are translated here, the love play between Rādhā and Kṛṣṇa progresses in several definite stages that reflect the emotional states of Rādhā as a heroine (nāyikā).[9]

At first, Rādhā prepares to receive her beloved. She decorates her body with sandal paste, red kumkum and fine clothes. In this emotional state she is a vāsakasajjā (ready to welcome her beloved). As time passes, and she sees no signs of her lover, she becomes anxious. This is the state of a virahotkaṇṭhitā (yearning for her beloved). Then slowly her lover approaches the trysting place she has prepared. The lovers are united. Now Rādhā becomes a svādhīna-patikā (united with her lover). In the course of their love play, the lovers quarrel over some small matter, and suddenly Rādhā's emotional state changes to that of a kalahāntaritā (divided in love).

In another set of circumstances, Rādhā prepares to meet her lover, but he does not come to her at all. She is overcome with grief and her emotional state is that of a vipralabdhā (overcome with sorrow waiting in vain for the lover). Later, she may discover that her lover had been to some other woman. At this, she becomes a khaṇḍitā (deceived).

Rādhā was married to another man, and so it sometimes happened that she could not meet her lover during the day. A night, she stealthily leaves her sleeping husband and goes out to meet

1. Narsī Mehtā's school; a cell in the second century A.D. Buddhist caves near Talaja, Bhavnagar.

2. The Gopnath Temple near Talaja.

3. The Dāmodara Temple and Tank (sixteenth century A.D.) at the foot of Girnar hills, Junagadh.

4. Śrī Nāthjī — Lord of Śrī (Lakṣmī)— Aspect of Kṛṣṇa worshipped at Nathdwara (Rajasthan), the principal seat of the Vallabhācārya sect. In this image, Kṛṣṇa stands with his left hand raised to hold Mount Govardhana (after a pichvāī painting).

5. The rāsa-dance (after a coloured lithoprint published by S. S. Brijbasi & Sons, Mathura, U.P.).

6. A Nathdwara pichvāi showing the rāsa-dance.

7. Veṇugopāla—Mysore style painting, late nineteenth century A.D.

her beloved. In this state, she is called an abhisārikā (one who leaves her home to meet her true lover).

The last emotional state of a proṣitabhartṛkā (one whose lover has gone away forever) is not described in the two set of love songs translated here. But in Narsī Mehtā's last work, *Govinda gamana*, Rādhā and all the gopīs of Vraja experience the emotional state of a proṣitabhartṛkā. The love affair between Rādhā and Kṛṣṇa as protrayed by Narsī Mehtā is throughout all the songs, clandestine. There is no attempt at making Rādhā a wife of Kṛṣṇa. Moreover, unlike the love poems of the Maithili poet Vidyāpati (born A.D. 1352), Narsī's Kṛṣṇa is always the dominant personality. Rādhā is a humble devotee. Following the bhakti idea that 'all souls are feminine to Lord Kṛṣṇa' Narsī frequently identifies himself with Rādhā. One special quality of all Narsī Mehtā's poems and songs—with the exception of *Surat sangrām*[10]—is that his descriptions of Rādhā-Kṛṣṇa love play never degenerate into pure eroticism. We are always made aware of the fact that the love play is symbolic of the union between the devotee and his God.

The Language of Narsī Mehtā

Narsī Mehtā does not refer to the language of his works as Gujarati. He calls it Apabhraṣṭa (fallen or changed). And yet, most of the songs and poems of Narsī Mehtā that are known to us are in a language not very different from the modern spoken Gujarati of the Saurashtra region. This means that his works have undergone considerable linguistic change. A simple comparison with the language of fifteenth century A.D. Jain *phāgus* (love-narratives) and *prabandhas* (historical tales), and the works of the poet Bhāḷaṇ (A.D. 1434-1514) will show how modern Narsī's language is.

One of the chief reasons for this linguistic change that Narsī Mehtā's works have suffered is their tremendous popularity. As most of his works are not careful, scholastic compositions, but spontaneous creations of a man deeply in love with Kṛṣṇa, they have a very direct appeal to people. Moreover, Narsī uses very few difficult Sanskrit words or sophisticated figures of speech.

This makes his works easily understood by the simple village folk. Many of Narsī's *rāsa* songs and *prabhātiyās* (morning songs) have become important part of Gujarati folk tradition. They are sung in villages even today. This great popularity meant that each generation would alter the language, and sometimes even the contents, of the poems to bring them into conformity with the language and customs of their time.

The followers of 'puṣṭi mārga'—founded by the south Indian Vaiṣṇava saint-philosopher Vallabhācārya—consider Narsī Mehtā to be a messenger (vadhaiyā) of their sect. Consequently, they have frequently altered many of Narsī's songs to make them conform with their beliefs and even to mention 'puṣṭi mārga' and the name of Vallabhācārya's son Viṭṭhalanātha (born A.D. 1518). To add to all these changes, a legend says that a poet called Lāl Kavi of Sayla, who considered himself to be an incarnation of Narsī Mehtā, wrote many poems under the latter's name. This makes it very difficult to judge the literary qualities of the works that have come down to us in the name of Narsī Mehtā. All that one can say is that Narsī's works are simple, direct and very popular. To him goes the credit of making poetry a living folk medium in Gujarat for the first time. It is for this reason that he is traditionally acclaimed to be the first (ādi) Gujarati poet.

NOTES

1. Viśvanāth Jāni's works are: (1) *Narsī Mehtā nun caritra* (life of Narsī Mehtā) which is incomplete, and (2) *Hār carit* (garland incident). The latter work has been published in *BKD*, part 8, pp. 609 ff. Premānand's works on the life of Narsī Mehtā are: (1) *Hār* (garland incident), (2) *Huṇḍī* (bond incident), (3) *Māmerun* (daughter's first pregnancy), (4) *Sāmaḷśā no vivāh* (wedding of son Śāmaḷśā), and (5) *Bāpnu śrāddha* (after-death rites of Narsī's father).

Premānand's works have been published many times, and in various editions. Both Jāni and Premānand rely as much on Narsī's autobiographical poems as they do on popular legends. There are many other minor biographers of Narsī, but they all take material either from Jāni or Premānand.

2. The traditional dates of Narsī Mehtā are given in the works of two early nineteenth century A.D. Gujarati poets, Vallabhadās and Mīṭhā Kavi. The sources of these dates are unknown.

3. An eighteenth century A.D. anonymous work called *Narsī Mehtānā*

Ākhyān (tales of Narsī Mehtā) says that Parvatdās did not die after Narsī's marriage, but left Talaja and lived to a very ripe old age in mangrol.

4. A legend says that Narsī adopted a new surname 'Diveṭīyo' (torch bearer) after the Gopnath experience and when he settled in Junagadh. It is difficult to establish the truth of this legend, but there are some songs in which the name 'Diveṭīyo' occurs instead of Narsī.

5. Mahatma Gandhi, in his reform movement, used this word to denote all the outcasts and untouchables of traditional Hindu society.

6. All the works of Narsī Mehtā are published in a collection called *Narsī Mehtā kṛt kāvya samgraha* by the Gujarati Printing Press, Bombay, in 1913, and edited by Icchārām Sūryarām Desāi.

7. There are actually 31 songs in the printed text, but one, number 24, has been omitted here as it is incomplete.

8. Rādhā is not mentioned by name in the *Bhāgavata Purāṇa.* She became popular as Kṛṣṇa's favourite consort in Gokula and Vraja only after Jayadeva's *Gīta-govinda.* The earliest mention of Rādhā, however, is in a Prakrit work entitled *Gāthā sattasāī* (1,89) by Hāla Sātavāhana (fifth century A.D.).

9. The emotional states that Rādhā experiences are all based on the traditional descriptions of the 'Nāyikā' that are common in the works of Sanskrit poetics. The list given here is an early one from the *Nāṭyaśāstra* (XXII, 97-98) of Bharata (first century A.D.).

10. This work has been considered by many scholars, in particular Shri K.K. Shastri as a later forgery, belonging to the group of so-called 'Baroda forgeries' (see K. M. Munshi, *Gujarat and Its Literature,* Bombay, 1967, pp. 195 and 276-77).

TRANSLATOR'S NOTE

This translation of the songs of Nasī Mehtā is a literal one. I have paid greater attention to translating the words and images into English rather than to any general interpretation of the spirit of the songs. I hope that the words of Narsī Mehtā will speak for themselves.

The songs of *Śṛṅgāra nā pado* and the philosophical/devotional (songs *Bhakti jñāna ane vairāgya nā pado*) are from *BKD*, part 1, pp. 5-16, and 18-25 and 29-30 respectively. The *Śṛṅgāra mālā* songs are published in *BKD*, part 2, pp. 18-28. The numbers in brackets, in songs 71-100, refer to the numbers in the printed text.

Each song is prefaced by a short note giving its meaning and general context.

ŚṚṄGĀRA NĀ PADO

[1 – 40]

Rādhā is deeply in love with Kṛṣṇa, who is no ordinary mortal, but Lord Viṣṇu incarnate. Generally, to get even a glimpse of God takes years of discipline and penance. But Kṛṣṇa comes easily to Rādhā on account of her intense love. This song stresses the bhakti doctrine that love for God far outweighs all other disciplines.

1

With what good deeds have I been born,
That the Lord himself should be lovelorn;
With great humility come to see,
And crave regards from only me.

The great immortals say the Lord
Cannot be won by wisdom's sword:
But yet that Lord who knows no check
Embraces me, arms round my neck.

The sacrifices, and the pain
Of penances, in which is sought in vain
A dream of Him who lives above,
That Lord I see with ease of love.

He leaves his restful Śeṣa[1] throne
From highest heaven he comes alone
To my abode—Love sanctified,
He, yellow-clad, comes to my bed.

The sacred texts say he fulfils
The promise, whom love so fills.
Narsī says Lord comes to me
Rewarding my humility.

[1]The serpent with a thousand heads on which Lord Viṣṇu rests during intervals of creation.

This song glorifies divine love, but emphasises the fact that love comes more easily to women (i.e. to the feminine personality) than to a man. As women like Rādhā and the gopīs could surrender completely to Kṛṣṇa, they were rewarded with salvation before male devotees were. This is the reason why many bhaktas, including the Tamil Āḷvār saints, looked upon themselves as maids of Kṛṣṇa.

2

Of all our incarnations, woman is supreme;
Balabhadra[1] is tamed by her.
Oh, sweet companion, what's the use
Of manly vigour in attaining my desire?

Salvation's path is granted to a man
If he is humble, and serves God.
But who the gentle, charming anger feels,
And flirting games, save woman that he loves?

Indra, the great sages, and the Formless One,
Do bow their heads to dust at gopīs' feet
Yet they consider You to be less great.
There son of Nanda's manliness shines not.

The wisdom and the truths from Vedānta,
The Vedas and the six Upaniṣads,
Are truly felt with ease and perfect joy
Each day, by only one—Your happy wife.

Like an animal on the road who, from bonds broke loose,
Tags on and follows; I cannot be lost.
Narsī's master Giridhara, the dark one,
Will grant his dreams. I fold my hands and bow.

[1]Kṛṣṇa's elder brother Balarāma.

Rādhā describes her love play with Kṛṣṇa in loving detail. She also says that being a woman, and deeply in love, she won the 'love battle' and Kṛṣṇa became her servant. This is probably a symbol of how the devotee can win over the Lord by sheer force of love.

3

This has been a wondrous fruitful night.
With me may darling sported on the bed.
With the excuse of seeing his reflected image.
In the mirror which I held, he kissed my cheek.

Wearing anklets and a garland made of flowers.
He embraced me, and pressed hard against my breast;
With my two hands I plunged into passion's battle
And won victory over Lord of Yadu clan.

I tested out the strength of Cupid's army;
The battle I indulged in I soon won.
I charmed, and then subdued, the Lord of fourteen worlds;
And gained merit quenching the unquenchable.

As the lioness, or elephant, in season.
Makes her mate dance to the orders that she gives,
Similarly Narsī's Lord, the God's great warrior,
Came to gopī's bed, where he did dance.

Kṛṣṇa and Rādhā have made love all night. Now it is day and their love play comes to an end. As usual, Kṛṣṇa has lost in the 'duel of love' and the devotee is the victor.

4

Are you not yet satisfied, with enjoyment of love play?
Four watches of the night we've passed, and it is now near day.

I drank the nectar of your lips, and not once did I say, no,
Nor from love's lion did I shrink, my back I did not show.

Armed with plump fleshy breasts, not fearing to advance,
Into love's hottest centre I went, glancing not askance.

I constantly, with hair and nails, took aim and did not miss
One chance to enhance desires' advance, not even by one kiss.

But now the sun has brought an end to love's long fought affray,
The intercourse which held its sway; Oh Narsī's Lord has lost this day.

Kṛṣṇa's foster mother Yaśodā looks upon him as an innocent child. The gods, and Brahmā, look upon him as the Lord of the universe. But to the gopīs of Vrindavana, Kṛṣṇa is the naughty, playful and amorous cowherd.

5

Oh Lord of Lakṣmī every day I see your ways of charm.
Yet your deceitful words and guile can do a grown-up's harm.

Your mother Yaśodā still says 'my little son's a pet'
But my beloved, everywhere you've worldly affairs set.

The One of whom the sages sing, whom Brahmā meditates,
Will not let any woman pass unless he with her mates.

But Oh dark Kṛṣṇa falter not in giving council here,
For Narsī has a great respect for all your women dear.

Rādhā tries to seduce little Kṛṣṇa into making love to her. She says she cares for no one else but Kṛṣṇa. This like the deep bhakti of the devotee who wants only the Lord and cares nothing for social conventions.

6

Beloved, you are small and we are young, a perfect match,
Give us your first embrace, and your first ecstasy we'll watch.

Women's nature's of such kind; they'll roam the world their love to find.
Embrace us as I now you bind, or we'll demand it of your mind.[1]

You are still young and so am I, my sister-in-law, her mother too,
Think of me as their little pet, yet try to stop me seeing you.

What can they do against such love, God's love has now so filled my heart
Oh Narsī's Lord what can I do, their worldly fears are so apart.

[1] i.e. Rādhā asks Kṛṣṇa to either voluntarily embrace her or she will force his to do so.

Kṛṣṇa comes to Rādhā. But he is surrounded by other young and beautiful gopīs. Rādhā would normally become jealous on seeing Kṛṣṇa with other gopīs. But her love for Kṛṣṇa won her over and she felt no jealousy. Instead she was delighted to be with the other gopīs, sporting with Kṛṣṇa.

7

When you came last night, my Lord, you were unsteady.
With intoxicated eyes you looked at me.
On either side you had a beautiful young woman,
Two others holding your hands and hanging round your neck.
So fine and handsome as you looked, it would be hard
To find anywhere in the universe a peer for you.

As I stood before you all jealousy vanished;
I just watched, surprised, the state and power of love.
I was pleased to see the good luck of your women.
The night was full of pleasure for my Lord.
Four women you were with, like lines of verses,[1]
And you gave their skirts your freedom to take leave.
When you lay abed, your shape did seem four sided.[2]
The gopīs you made happy with love play.

Narsī says that love is fresh where merits
Of Govinda are sung; and what does Brahmā know
(Who is too full of power and its troubles)
Of divine love, as is to women shown.

[1]Like four verses make one poem, so four gopis and one Kṛṣṇa were like one couple.

[2]Though Kṛṣṇa was alone and there was four gopis, each gapi felt that Kṛṣṇa was with her alone.

Kṛṣṇa was known for his amorous nature. He was loved by all the gopīs of Vrindavana. Rādhā sometimes became jealous of Kṛṣṇa's promiscuity. In such moods, she would tie him up to punish him. Narsī, the poet, takes Kṛṣṇa's side and requests Rādhā not to be harsh to the divine child.

8

Throwing all shame to the winds, she tied his hands up tight
With flower garland, to the bed support.
There is no point, she said, for you to struggle or to shọut
For there is none to come and help you in my house.

You are like the gardener, and I the flowering plant;
Why don't you regularly water me ?
Like a bee you go from flower to flower, and never stop for long;
Why can't your only love the lotus[1] be?

The one who really loves would place his body, mind, and life
Only at the feet of his loved one.
But Narsī says, Oh Gopī please, say kind words alone
And let your anger lessen and grow cool.

[1]Meaning Rādhā.

Kṛṣṇa pleads with Rādhā to untie him and let him go free. He promises to be with her always and not to run after other gopīs. He even promises her salvation. Finally Rādhā sets him free and they sport with each other.

9

'I will not come to your house again, O Amorous One,' young Kṛṣṇa shouts.

'You are mean and cowardly, that is why you tied me up with flowers.

In fact you are the flowering plant, and I am the gardener.[1]

I look at you with lust filled eyes, and water you with hands;

So I in fact should bind you up, enclosing you with love.

I know your love charms worked on me, but listen Beauteous One:

I promise from rebirths you're freed if you will loose my bonds.

Be pleased, Oh Proud One, see I beg with all humility.

I swear I'll never leave your house.' With such words did he plead.

In this way Narsī's Lord expresses emotions in full range,

And she succeeds in making him obedient in love play.

[1]This is a pun on the similarity between the Sanskrit word Vanamālī (wearer of a garland of forest flowers) and the Gujarati word mālī (gardener).

According to the tradition of Jayadeva's *Gita govinda*, Rādhā was a parakīyā nāyikā—the one who belonged to another. Her love for Kṛṣṇa was illicit. So she visited him secretly at night. They made love all night, but as soon as it was daylight Rādhā had to be back in her house before her in-laws woke up. In this song, Kṛṣṇa is sleepy and does not want Rādhā to go. Rādhā threatens never to come to him again if he does not let her go. Hearing this, Kṛṣṇa loosens his hold and lets her go. As soon as she has left Kṛṣṇa, she begins to feel the pain of separation.

10

'Oh Yellow-clad One let go my clothes,
The sun is up, how can I sleep?
My strict in-laws will question me,
My husband too, what could I say?

Daylight makes the lamps glow faint,
The animals make waking sounds,
Your flower garland's withered now
And I can hear the fifth note sound.[1]

Sleep is easy now for Lakṣmī's Lord,
In the peaceful comfort of his house.
I have far to go where people see,
And in their eyes I've lost respect.

I've cows to milk, and calves to feed,
More work to do then, churning milk.
I will not come to you again !'
At this, her lover loosed his hold.

And so the amorous play did close
Narsī's Lord went straight to sleep.
I, left with sleepless night, and heavy head,
And in my heart was separation's pain.

[1]The song of kokilā (*Eudynamis scolopaceus*), the Indian cuckoo. This is a dark coloured bird common in mango gardens during the flowering season, and is believed to produce the exact fifth (pañcama) note.

At first Kṛṣṇa plays hard to get, but seeing the true love of Rādhā, he goes to her house to make love to her all night.

11

Do not give me guileful words—
Just come home with me.
No more arrogance from you—
Just come home with me.

I want to hear from you no lies,
I know your true intent.
All night, being charmed, we played at love,
Dawn is now near.

The love marks on your body show,
I fear the elders' wrath;
But Narsī's master visits me,
So should I not give praise ?

The nightly love-making of Rādhā and Kṛṣṇa is discovered one morning when Kṛṣṇa leaves his yellow cloth on Rādhā's bed and takes away her bed-cover. Rādhā is punished and not allowed to go out of the house. But she longs to see Kṛṣṇa like a true devotee who longs for the Lord.

12

We went to bed at twilight, under covers there we lay;
But my *nanand*[1] called next morning and my Lord was scared away.
Kṛṣṇa's yellow garment was left lying on the floor,
My bracelet and bed-cover he fled with through the door.
My elders punished me so hard for being with my Lord,
How can I now go to sell curds and milk abroad?
Meeting Narsī's Lord, I'm sure, from rebirths sets one free.
With aching jaw and burning limbs where can my pride now be?

[1]Husband's sister (i.e. sister-in-law).

Rādhā cares no longer what her family or her in-laws say about her love for Kṛṣṇa. She is so much in love that she just does not care for social consequences of her actions. This is the plight of most bhaktas, including Narsī Mehtā. They have to choose between God and the world, and they usually take the former, as Rādhā did, and have to bear the torments of the world.

13

You try to hide when going from me
Try to hide then disappear.
You cannot go till you embrace me,
Let my wicked *nanad* hear.

I have no fear of wicked words,
Let parents, in-laws, my name smear.
Many times such things I've heard.
I cannot leave you now my dear.

Sweet nectar of your love, my Lord,
Only the great yogis knew.
By Śuka's Sanakādi's words[1]
And in the Vedas, your praise grew.

Nārada and Jayadeva,
Girls of Vraja[2] knew your love.
The world had lost that divine flavour,
Narsī's saved it with his love.

[1]Śuka was the son of Vyāsa, the traditional author of the *Mahābhārata* and the *Purāṇas*. Sanakādi (lit. Sanaka etc.) includes Sanaka, Sanandana and Sanatkumāra—three sons of Brahmā.

[2]A pastoral district near Mathura, where Kṛṣṇa spent most of his childhood.

Narsī Mehtā describes the beautiful scene where Kṛṣṇa and the gopī Rādhā have come to Nanda's house after playing with colour. They both look so beautiful that no one can decide who is greater, Kṛṣṇa or Rādhā—the devotee or the Lord.

14

Both wet with saffron colour
Stood the gopī and her Lord,
With eyes brim-full of love, they were
Standing at Nanda's[1] door.

Which one is more beautiful
The lady or her love?
Value them as you would
Two rubies beyond price.

Sparklingly, with graceful gait,
They swiftly walk along
To the bower of thick creepers twined,
And there make endless love.
'Oh ! what a wondrous sight it is'
Says Narsī in his joy.

[1]Kṛṣṇa's foster father and a rich cowherd.

The magical flute of Kṛṣṇa bewitched all the women of Gokula and Vrindavana. As soon as they heard the flute they became hypnotised.

15

By your graceful movements my mind is bewitched,
Oh I am bewitched by your playful mood.
Oh Bearer of Mountains,[1] my limbs are quite numb
As if hit by a blow, I am stunned.

With such charm in the forest he played on his flute
That my mind only thought of the saffron-clad one.
Whilst playing with Narsī's young Lord I was stung
With an increase of passion—my mind was bewitched.

[1]Giridhārī, one of the many names of Kṛṣṇa.

Rādhā describes the state of her mind which is overcome with love for Kṛṣṇa. Sleep and hunger have left her and every minute she pines for his return. This state of mind is similar to that of a true devotee when not lost in ecstasy.

16

You are enchanting Oh ! Dark One
You are enchanting me.
You have so captivated me
With your seductive charm
That I have lost, entirely lost,
The calmness of my mind.
You are enchanting Oh ! Dark One.

Seeing the state of mind I'm in
My mother-in-law grieves,
My sister-in-law ridicules
And looks reproachfully.
You are enchanting Oh ! Dark One.

I have no appetite for food
And sleep has left me quite,
You are enchanting Oh ! Dark One.

You have tied my feet with a coil of rope
And with your lips have made me red.
You are enchanting Oh ! Dark One.

I have reached the highest heaven
In finding Narsī's Lord,
You are enchanting Oh ! Dark One.

Rādhā, or perhaps one of the other gopīs, describes with joy Kṛṣṇa's visit to her house.

17

Come, leave your red footprints,[1] my king,

Come with red footprints,
Diffusing strong and fragrant perfume,
Come with dancing steps
And leave your red footprints.

With turbaned head you look so fine,
Your shoulder cloth of green.
Your yellow dhoti round your waist,
Your face shows pearl-like drops of toil.
To look at you is to lose all peace of mind—
Come, leave your red footprints.

On my house now falls all the sweet
Of nectar, honeydew.
The rain is milk, the glistening drops
Are sweet in Narsī's view.
Come, leave your red footprints, my king.
Come, leave your red footprints.

[1]This refers to the custom of colouring the feet young girls and boys with either kumkum or henna.

The gopīs insist that Kṛṣṇa show equal love and attention to all of them. If he shows any partiality, they threaten to expose his naughty games to his mother Yaśodā.

18

I know the secret of your heart
O Giridhara, collector of dues.
My companion has seen what you do
With a group of young friends down the street.

Consider the gopīs equally
Oh my beloved, do not prefer
One to another, as milk is preferred to whey,
Or Nanda's wife shall hear of your play.

While on my way to Vrindavan[1]
My colourful saree he pulled from me.
I was playing with Narsī's Lord,
Now my heart is deeply enveloped in love.

[1] A wood on the banks of the Yamunā river in the district of Mathura, where Kṛṣṇa played with the gopīs.

In this song, the gopīs describe Kṛṣṇa's pranks. Whenever they go out to fetch water from the river or to sell milk, Kṛṣṇa stops them, sometimes breaks their pots or steals their butter. But the real, and deep, reason for all this complaining is to remember the Lord.

19

Kṛṣṇa, collector of dues, always stops me.
I shall not fetch water from Jamunā's bank.
Once I went, but that time my companion was with me,
I will not go alone to the Jamunā's edge.

One time on the way to Vrindavan he stopped me
And took my expensive new saree away,
So if you must send me to fetch any water
Be sure that you send a companion with me.

That thief has now stolen my heart from me,
And to his temptation have I fallen prey.
With Narsī's master I played and sported,
So now he is part of me, both night and day.

Rādhā compares the beauty of Vrindavana to the joys of heaven, and concludes that Vrindavana is better. Heaven may be place of eternal joy but it is dead place without love. Vrindavana may not be perfect, but people here are full of love.

20

My Vrindavan's beauty your Vaikuṇṭha[1] cannot excel
Without food or drink I set here,
At Vrindavan I will stay.
You may send celestial chariots
Thinking I'll be first to come,
But I will not come to Vaikuṇṭha
No I will not see your home.

Inhabitants of Brahmā's heaven are all heartless, so I hear,
But the people of Vraja
Are so kind and full of love,
That even if, without a warning,
Your door-keepers were dismissed,[2]
I should still prefer my Vraja
Where the people are love kissed.

Śārṅgapāṇi[3] listen, for I tell you now in truth,
I shall not, no, never shall I, come to you in your Vaikuṇṭha.

[1]The paradise of Viṣṇu.
[2]The door-keepers of paradise prevent unsanctioned souls from entering.
[3]The one who holds in his hand (pāṇi) the bow called Śārṅga; one of the 1000 names of Viṣṇu.

When divine love reaches its highest point, the devotee feels one with the Lord. This is the state of Rādhā who feels that even though Kṛṣṇa is not physically with her all the time, they are one, and therefore always together.

21

We are joined as one forever, my king !
I feel your stirrings in each part of me.
Not for one second are we separate hearts,
You are my slender love, my life and soul,
You are before my eyes both night and day.
When I look through the door I see you stand,
When I look through the window there you sit.
Even in the street you walk with me.

Oh Darling sweet, surpassing nectar's taste !
When I sit down to eat, you sup with me,
When I lie down to sleep, you rest with me,
And on my daily way to Vrindavana
You come and take the pails of milk from me.
You never leave alone the one you love
But giving such voluptuous ecstasy,
Has Narsī's master made my heart his home.

Rādhā requests the moon not to set and let daylight come. She is with Kṛṣṇa, making love, and at sunrise they will be separated. Rādhā says that she has waited and prayed for many births just to be born in Gokula, near Kṛṣṇa. Now that they are together, they do not want to be parted. They want the night to go on forever.

According to the *Padma* and *Nārada Purāṇas*, Rādhā lived in Vaikuṇṭha where she performed austere penances to become Viṣṇu's beloved. When Viṣṇu incarnated as Kṛṣṇa, she was born as Rādhā. According to the Puṣṭi mārga doctrine of Vallabhācārya, Rādhā was an incarnation of the goddess Lakṣmī.

22

Wait ! Wait ! Oh moon, do not let day break now.
My life's beloved, life and soul, has come,
The ornament of manhood now is here
To quench my previous births' long felt desire.

The Lord of fourteen worlds, in my past life,
Was my beloved; but to attain again
The same sweet love, much penance have I done.
Take pity on my plight. Wait ! Wait ! Oh moon.

I lie here and hear the cātaka bird sing.[1]
The charming song of cuckoo now I hear,
But cockerel utter not your dreaded sound
In case you break the morn. Wait ! Wait ! Oh moon.

Oh companion mine of graceful gait;
I lay at night all wrapped around Govinda,
As cool and pale moonlight wraps round the moon,
Entwined like creeper's tendrils. Wait ! Wait ! Oh moon.

The motions Narsī's Lord made in my bed,
That one Govinda whom all the gopīs love,
Resembled actions of the sea's high waves.
Oh let the night go on. Wait ! Wait ! Oh moon.

[1]See note on song 33.

This song follows the famous 'gopikā gītā' of the *Bhāgavata Purāṇa*. Kṛṣṇa, who was playing with the gopīs, suddenly disappears. The gopīs are overcome with the pain of separation. They look for Kṛṣṇa all around. They search for clues, they find his footprints, they ask the trees and creepers for Kṛṣṇa's whereabouts. They finally decide to kill themselves if Kṛṣṇa does not come. Eventually, the compassionate Lord comes to make the gopīs happy.

23

I search for you in every street
And endlessly I look
For footprints of the yellow clad.
So mad I am with passion filled,
My footsteps are unsteady.
So fast I run like a frightened doe,
I lose my sense for love of you.

I seek the Dark One everywhere
With teardrops in my eyes,
Which with my clothes I wipe away,
As with the Gopīs I decide
Young Nanda's haunts to find.
We walked to river Jamunā's bank
And pointed to a place
Where Hari sat to eat sweet rice,
And there he played his flute,
Here on this spot he sang with us
Of love we'll not forget.

We asked the creepers if they knew
Of any news of you.
Our Lord has left us, gone away
In the guise of common herd.

Our cherished bodies—youthful, sweet—
We will give our king.
If soon we cannot Hari find,
We'll sacrifice our lives.

To this same spot we'll come again
And yet again we'll come.
We blessed count his human form—
We know that in this shape
The possibility is near
Of knowing Nanda's son.

We even asked the sea if it
Had seen Narsī's dear Lord.
The Lord of all the humble ones,
The beloved compassionate one.

Rādhā invites Lord Kṛṣṇa to come to the woods of Vrindavana to spend the time in amorous play.

24

Come, come, my sweetly speaking Lord,
Come to some lonely place awhile
And I shall tell the secrets of my heart.

Today my heart in happiness abounds,
For my beloved touched my hand with love.
Today my dear will bear auspicious marks,
And all night long will I sing songs of love.

In leafy nooks and paths of Vrinda's trees,
Did Narsī's master play love games 'til dawn.

Kṛṣṇa was spent the night with Rādhā in her house, unknown to anyone else. Now it is dawn and Rādhā has to do her house work. Before anyone else in the house awakes, Kṛṣṇa must leave. So Rādhā gently requests the sleeping Kṛṣṇa to let her go.

25

Yaśodā's son please let me rise.
My clothes are 'neath your head.
Oh let me get my clothes, my love.
Just roll over in the bed.

All my companions wait for me,
To go and fetch the water.
The birds all sing, the night has gone.
Wake now, then sleep on after.

Oh ! if I shout to wake you up,
The other folks might hear.
I cannot even move my feet
For the toe-bells that I wear.

I hear them churning milk next door,
So any moment now
My envious sister-in-law will rise,
Then there will be a row !

Of cause, effect, I am aware.
Desires bring their reward.
How could I ever see this dawn
Without Narsī's dear Lord.

The gopīs admire Kṛṣṇa's dark, handsome beauty. They cannot resist him. They are like the cows that are stealthily milked by Kṛṣṇa but cannot resist him.

26

Mohana stands on Jamunā's bank,
Plays his melodious flute.
He looks so handsome standing there
With yellow cloth around his waist
And shining jewels at ears and throat.

At dawn the gopīs milk the cows,
And call the Dark One's name.
The cows give very little milk
The Dark One's been before.
One gopī says to all her friends
'The cows are drained by *Him*, like us'.

Hearing these words, the gopīs thrilled
With happiness, to think
That Narsī Methā's Lord and love,
Had so accepted them.

This song is basically theistic, and stresses the omnipresent nature of Lord Kṛṣṇa. A gopī, perhaps Rādhā, binds baby Kṛṣṇa up and puts him in a large pot. Then, in order to advertise that she has eventually managed to punish the naughty Kṛṣṇa by imprisoning him in a pot, she pretends to sell him. Then she hears the sound of Kṛṣṇa's magical flute coming from the woods. She cannot believe that Kṛṣṇa has escaped and so looks in the pot to confirm that he is still there. To her great surprise, instead of baby Kṛṣṇa bound up, she sees a vision of the entire cosmic order including Kṛṣṇa, and herself, in the pot. This incident is similar to another incident where Kṛṣṇa reveals the entire universe in his mouth to his mother Yaśodā.

27

After putting Hari, loved of gopīs by the score,
Into a pot of earthenware she went from door to door,
Offering to sell the Lord of all the world, she cried,
'Who wants to buy Murāri[1], that is who is here inside'.

This simple shepherdess then heard the sounding of a flute.
She put the pot down, looked inside. The vision made her mute,
For Kṛṣṇa was inside, in bed, beside the Vraja girl!
Brahmā, Indra, others too come peeping in a whirl,
They were surprised to see the Lord of all the fourteen worlds
Inside a little earthen pot. With laughter they were curled.
The shepherdess was lucky though to see the Omniscient
Lord of Narsī who so rewards the humble penitent.

[1]Enemy (ari) of the demon Murā': One of the many names of Kṛṣṇa.

This song describes the state of Rādhā's mind. She has fallen in love with Kṛṣṇa. She cannot understand how this happened, but now she has no desire for anything else but Kṛṣṇa. This state of mind compares with the state of a true bhakta who has intense devotion for God.

28

Once having seen the beloved,
I am quite satisfied.
How can I ever stay at home
When on him I have laid my eye.

The face of my beloved one
Has so enchanted me,
That I am sure he cast a spell
Or love charm over me.

All the joy in worldly life has gone.
His charming image has
Entered my body as his own.
He knows now my desires.

I feel to him I am now chained
With chains af purest gold.
Darling you and I are one—
To Narsī's Lord all praise !

Rādhā and Kṛṣṇa meet and make love in the jasmine covered bowers of Vrindavana. Rādhā feeds him sweets and milk products and Kṛṣṇa promises her everlasting joy.

29

My arbour is covered with jasmine today,
Rādhā's dark darling has come for love play.

Kṛṣṇa is dark skinned and Rādhā is fair,
When they play the bells ring that are tied in her hair.

My darling takes sweet curds, milk, sweets made of bājra,[1]
Made and offered with love by the hands of the gopī.

The gopī with suitable ornaments covered,
Enjoyed Viṭṭhala's[2] advances in Vrindavana covert.[3]

Narsī's Lord gave me the wristband of marriage,
With my handsome husband, death cannot disparage.

[1]A millet.

[2]The name under which Kṛṣṇa is worshipped in Pandharpur on the banks of the Bhīmā river in Maharashtra.

[3]Meaning a nest or bower.

Kṛṣṇa usually attracts the gopīs by playing his magical flute which no one on earth can resist. Whatever the gopīs are busy with, as soon as they hear the flute, their passions are aroused and they come rushing out to meet him.

30

Someone sang the sweet fifth rāga[1]
Near my house.
Suddenly my love rushed in
And grabbed me by the hand.

He looked so handsome standing there,
Yellow cloth around his waist;
With jewelled neck and golden crown.
His passion grew as he looked on.

To raise my passion to his own,
He played his flute for me.
Then with deep love my darling held
And pressed me to his breast.

Then he came into my house
And there he enjoyed me.
Narsī says that she now gained
Most complete happiness.

[1]Pañcama, an afternoon Rāga of northern Indian music intended to arouse erotic feeling.

Rādhā and Kṛṣṇa play love games. They swing together and swim in the Yamunā river. They invite all the gopīs to join them and then they all play with Kṛṣṇa.

31

Of love and passion I am full,
When with the Dark One on the swing.
He also shows me his desire.
I give him long embraces.

While swinging to and fro he plays
Love games with me, then later on
We dance together in a ring,
He fondles me with pleasure.

Companions, come to Jamunā
To swim there with our Lord.
Whilst swimming our bare bodies touch
And furtively he kisses me.

Come, let me rock you on the swing,
Sing love songs till you sleep.
Sporting like this with Narsī's Lord,
My arms around his neck.

This song describes the love play of Rādhā and Kṛṣṇa as they swing together.

32

I and my darling were on the swing swaying
When he became filled with quick passion for me.
The beautiful one[1] then felt shyness no longer.

The beautiful woman, the passionate Kṛṣṇa—
Onlookers would think they were husband and wife.
Whilst swinging their bodies came into close contact
And each felt a tickling right down their spine.

Cupid affected the Lord of the humble,
Who is also the master of Narsī's poor heart,
And the proud one[2] was also then filled with pure love.

[1]and [2]Both these adjectives refer to Rādhā.

The rainy season is considered to be the season for the reunion of lovers. But Rādhā waits in vain for Kṛṣṇa to come. He does not come and Rādhā is tormented. All the beauties of nature remind her of Kṛṣṇa and therefore give her no pleasure. This is the state of a devotee separated from his beloved Lord. Rādhā is here a khaṇḍitā nāyikā.

33

The rainy season of love is here,
But my master has not yet returned.
Cupid, the hunter is ready with shafts,
How can I make love, all alone?

Lightning flashes and clouds roar,
The rain is pouring down.
Where is my love at such a time?
My Lord is ungrateful, what can I do?

The days of separation pain me.
Frogs' and peacocks' sounds I fear.
I am mad with separation's torment,
The cātaka[1] bird-cry now banishes sleep.

Absence of Narsī' Lord, sweet Hari,
Is like misfortune's heavy fall.
Those who feel not thus for Hari
Are like beasts, not men at all.

[1]*Cuculus melanoleucas*: a swallow like bird, which in legend is said to drink only raindrops as they fall from the clouds.

In this song, Rādhā and Kṛṣṇa are united. As it is rainy season, Rādhā, Kṛṣṇa and all the cowherd girls and boys dance and sing. Nature rejoices with them.

34

To the thunder of rain clouds, Mādhava dances,
The bells on his ankles all ring.
The gopīs keep time with cymbals and drum-beat
And Kṛṣṇa then makes his flute sing.

The gopīs are dressed up in pink silken sarees,
Cātakas, peacocks and frogs are all singing.
The cuckoo joins in then to make up a chorus
And to the fine music, He melody brings.

Bless'd are the flute and the banks of the Jamunā,
Vrindavana's incarnation is blessed too.
Bless'd is the tongue of the singer named Narsī
Who sang rāga Malhār so clear and true.

When two people are in love, they may quarrel and sometimes argue. They may even use abusive language to each other. Such love quarrels were frequent between Rādhā and Kṛṣṇa. But they were secret and no one else knew about them. Here, Rādhā requests Kṛṣṇa not to use abusive language and make public their secret love affair. Any hint that Kṛṣṇa was on intimate terms with Rādhā could cause a scandal in her house.

35

If you abuse me with your language
All will know we are in love;
Therefore darling, I beseech you
Do not abuse me with your tongue.

You burst into my house a-cursing
Disguised as a godly beggar,[1]
Be careful, do not press me roughly.
My husband is uneasy, anxious,
He will surely seek the truth.
He will discover we are familiar.
Do not abuse me with your tongue.

My envious sister-in-law will find out.
She will scold me very hard.
Narsī's Lord, I tell you truly,
I shall be banished from the house.
Do not abuse me with your tongue.

[1]A sādhu, religious mendicant.

Kṛṣṇa and the gopīs play with colour to celebrate the festival of holi. But Kṛṣṇa sometimes gets too rough and then the gopīs become angry. To get back at him, they complain about his past misconduct; the days when he took advantage of their love for him to steal their milk and curds.

36

How can we continue to live in Vrindavana?
Nanda's young Narahari[1] robs everyone.
He treats all us gopīs so roughly,
Holding my feelings for him to ransom.

He breaks all our pots and spills all the milk,
To one he speaks with suggestive, sly words.
With another he rows and shaws he is angry.
How can we go through the forest-paths now?

From one of us gopīs he tears the fine garments,
From another he snatches her bodice away.
He pushes some roughly while others he plays with,
Throwing water and soaking us from head to toe.

In such ways as described here, sporting and playful,
Narsī's Lord, colourful always in play,
Plays holi,[2] and dances with girls from Vrindavana,
Dances and plays with them all through the day.

[1]Hari (Viṣṇu) in human (nara) form, i.e. Kṛṣṇa.

[2]A popular, and very ancient spring festival of northern India. This is celebrated three days before the full moon of phālguna (February-March) by throwing coloured powders and liquids at people.

Rādhā is temporarily separated from Kṛṣṇa. So she refuses to wear make-up and good clothes. She also advises other gopīs not to try and impress Kṛṣṇa with mere show. This advice appiles equally to those devotees who think that religious marks and empty ritual will please the Lord.

37

Many women colour their eyes with collyrium,
My case is different from all of theirs.
I have thrown off all ornaments and aids to beauty
Until my lover once more calls me near.

You cannot please Kṛṣṇa with mere show;
If you try you will be like a flower without scent.
Which, having no perfume, no person will wear,
Which though lovely to see, has no substance inside.

One gains favour with Kṛṣṇa with pure heart and mind,
He loves the faithful and the true.
The essence of Narsī's Lord goes very deep,
I can taste little of it in this mortal sleep.

Rādhā is deeply in love with Kṛṣṇa and with the melody of his sweet music. This music is like a love spell to her.

38

Now my mind belongs to Śyāma,[1]
By his eyes I am bewitched,
I utter his name only,
Kān[2] has put his spell on me.

As the cry of the gentle deer
Pierces the ears of the loving doe,
So am I pierced by the music
Of Govinda's flute and song.

It one loves a lilting melody,
If gives pleasure to the ear,
Similarly Narsī's heart is pleased
Drinking the nectar of Hari's name.

[1]Śyāma=dark; an adjective meaning Kṛṣṇa.
[2]Kān is colloquial Gujarati for Kṛṣṇa.

Like a true devotee, Rādhā wants none else in the entire universe but her beloved Kṛṣṇa.

39

There is only one I love,
I have love for only one.
The beloved of the gopīs
Is the only one I love.

I have no need for any other,
On my father's head I swear.
After getting Nanda's son
I shall have no further care.

The sight of handsome Kṛṣṇa,
Gives deep pleasure to my heart.
Who forsakes him for another
Does a deed as black as coal.

He is like a fop or dandy,
Yet has virtues by the score,
Narsī's dark complexioned master,
Lord of Vaiṣṇavas, and All.

Though Rādhā is married to another man, when Kṛṣṇa comes secretly to her house, she forgets all the bonds of family and society and welcomes him as if he were husband. They sport together all night and experience supreme bliss.

40

Quietly, silently, hari enters my house.
To welcome him I scatter large shiny pearls.
He has enchanted and bewitched me,
He has robbed me of my heart.
I lay awake watching for a glimpse of Hari's face.
Now gone are all the troubles of my life.
I rejoiced and was delighted to see Hari's handsome face,
I have forgotten and discarded all the burdens of the house,
I have reached the highest place, I have achieved a place in heaven,
I have met, I have attained the master, Narsī Mehtā's Lord.

ŚṚṄGĀRA MĀLĀ

[41–70]

Kṛṣṇa has spent the night with another gopī, leaving Rādhā alone. Next morning Kṛṣṇa comes to Rādhā. She is jealous, and sarcastically welcomes him asking him where he had spent the night. Finally, she requests him never to go to another gopī. Here Rādhā is at first a khaṇḍitā nāyikā (deceived) and then a svādhīnapatikā nāyikā (united with her love).

41

Welcome Mohana my beloved
Most promiscuous of lovers;
You have been gone for too long.
Which house did you visit before ?

You have now a new-found habit
Of visiting others' abodes
There is no way I can stop you,
Where shall I find solace now?

To prevent public contempt
Please stop pursuing this course.
Narsī's Lord, take warning from me:
If this is found out, honour's lost.

This song has the same theme as song 41. Kṛṣṇa has deceived Rādhā and spent the night elsewhere. He comes to her next morning. At first Rādhā is angry and jealous, but seeing Kṛṣṇa she melts and her anger vanishes. She greets Kṛṣṇa with love.

42

Tell me O Dark One, tell me my love,
Forsaking your favourite, where did you go?
Abandoned by you I shed tears all night.
The long nights of loneliness I cannot bear.

You very well know, without you I would die
Yet you suddenly leave me and reject my love.
All the words which you spoke with such charm
and such guile
Whilst we were in bed, you seem now to forget.

Your behaviour is selfish, like that of someone
Who makes the doctor his enemy once he is cured.
But when Narsī's master comes back to my house
I greet him with honour and ceremony.
His presence brings happiness and joy to me.

Rādhā prepares to receive Kṛṣṇa. She dresses herself and decorates the trysting place. She becomes a vāsakasajjā nāyikā (ready to welcome her beloved).

43

The Dark One ornaments my heart
I want him near always.
To look at him, his charming form,
A sight that all speech allays.

I decorate my body now
With jewels very fine,
Prepare for him a nice soft bed
And trim the lamps to shine.

I spread eye-shadow in my eyes
Used gestures very few,
Though keen to play with Narsī's Lord,
At this approach, I timid grew.

Kṛṣṇa comes to Rādhā who is waiting to receive him. The sight of the beloved approaching fills her with longing. Here Rādhā is a svādhīnapatikā nāyikā (united with her lover).

44

With love my handsome lover comes
To satisfy my longing.
Seeing the loved one of my heart
I dance with joy and sing.

The sight of my beloved approaching
Fills me with such joy
My body cannot now contain
The joy that flows within.

With jewelled body, perfumed hair,
I rush to welcome him;
I light the lamp within the house
Soon Narsī's master's sport begins.

Rādhā and quarrelled with Kṛṣṇa—state of a kalahāntaritā nāyikā (divided in love). Now Narsī requests Rādhā to go to Kṛṣṇa, to abandon pride, and to seduce him into making love.

45

Abandon pride ! Give in to love,
Do all you can to please.
Make loving gestures to Śyāma
And gently embrace him.

With nectar flowing from your eyes
Look on his handsome face.
When Cupid's darts have spurred you on
Hold him in close embrace.

If your love gestures urge you on
And he shows passions true,
Your womanhood is then complete
So Narsī says to you.

Kṛṣṇa has a reputation for being mischievous. He steals the gopīs' clothes when they go to bathe in the river; he snatches their gold ornaments and throws colour on them. In this song, the gopīs request him not to subject them to his usual pranks.

46

Nanda's darling has great charm
But when bathing, beware harm.
The Lord of Yādavas I see
Standing beneath a kadamba[1] tree.
Your cowherdesses, so demure,
I know will not be secure.

Dark One do not hold my bangle,
In your desire with me to tangle.
For you it is play
But it would blacken my whole day.
The bangle is made of solid gold
And is an heirloom, very old.

Kṛṣṇa ! Do not throw red colour on us
You will soil our hair and dress.
We shall have to then explain
To our elders, who'll complain.

The sports of Narsī's Lord Śrī Kṛṣṇa
Adorned with jewels, and with Rādhā
All bedecked with pearls
Give salvation's joy to worlds.

[1] *Anthocephalus cadamba*: This tree is said to put forth buds at the roaring of thunder clouds.

After a lovers' quarrel Kṛṣṇa neither comes to see Rādhā nor talks to her. Rādhā has become a kalahāntaritā nāyikā (divided in love). She is overcome with grief but she cannot get the handsome form of Kṛṣṇa out of her mind and she longs for him. Therefore, Rādhā is also a virahotkaṇṭhitā nāyikā (yearning for the beloved).

47

My Lord will not speak to me,
His silence is killing me.
How can I endure such pain?
My friends, I implore you
Show me how to bear this abandonment's pain ?

He abandons me utterly.
When catching sight of me
Turns his back on me,
Evading my gaze.
What can I do for I'm dying to meet him ?

On his crown, a bright feather,
At his hips yellow cloth,
Sparkling gold earrings,
How handsome he is.
If only I could see
The master of Narsī
My life's aim would then be
Wholly fulfilled.

This song is very much like songs 41 and 42. Rādhā is jealous because she has been deceived (khaṇḍitā) by Kṛṣṇa who has spent the night with another gopī. Rādhā greets Kṛṣṇa with sarcastie words.

48

Today your body is weary, on account of your night's toil.
Why then have yon come to my house, have you lost the way to her's ?
Do not tell me you have left your new companion all alone.

I suppose that red dye has rubbed off on you from her hands and feet.
And her forehead mark looks lovely on your lips.
I see that drops of sweat now make your golden earrings shine,
And your eyes are dazed with longing for your love.

Having left your yellow garment, you now wear a green saree;
Your lips are all besmudged with eye-shadow.
Tell me Lord, who is that beauteous one who did not sleep last night
In her eagerness to entertain you so ?

You are welcome so early at the break of day,
I only hope your longings are no more.
But tell me darling libertine, what is this woman's name
Who causes me such sorrow and such shame?

Tell me, my lifelong love, what she has that I do not ?
Is she far less proud than I, is that not it ?
I advise you Narsī's Lord that you must begin to change your ways
Your adulterousness is worthy of no praise.

Rādhā has spent a night of love making with Kṛṣṇa. Her body is marked with bites and scratches. Now that it is day, Rādhā is worried about what people will say when they see her body covered with love-marks.

The third and fourth stanzas of this song suddenly become philosophical. They interpret the Rādhā-Kṛṣṇa love affair symbolically. Kṛṣṇa, who is an incarnation of Lord Viṣṇu, only appears to make love. In actual fact he is beyond all desires and is a celibate. And Rādhā is a symbol of the bhakta.

49

Release your hold upon my saree
It is daylight now dear Hari,
I hear people make faint sounds
Soon my sister-in-law will come round.

I came to your bed last night, early,
And we embraced the night through tightly.
My body is now covered
With your nail marks, and I'm as bothered
About your teeth-marks on my lips.
Who sees me now will say with quips
These are surely signs of passion
And adultery is my fashion.

Says Kṛṣṇa 'Hear my lover,
I am celibate forever.
There are few who know the real me.
Sanakādi and Nārada
Can only praise the son of Nanda
My mystery evades them totally'.

'The Vedas have not known me,

And in them I am quite lonely.[1]
Only gopīs and the poets
Solve my mystery and know it
And on earth today, just Narsī
Can untangle my real mystery.'

[1]This refers to the doctrine of Viṣṇusvāmin and Vallabhācārya which states that the Primeval Soul was lonely, and so desiring to be many, became the Universe and all the individual souls in it. It is likely that the third and fourth stanzas are later additions.

This song describes how Rādhā is seduced by Kṛṣṇa and how her love for him becomes deep and enduring. Rādhā compares Kṛṣṇa's sudden movements to the movements of a snake.

50

Where are you going, Oh ! young woman ?
Your footsteps are unsure
And your body shakes. Has someone seduced you?
Or are you bitten by a snake,
Or perhaps some drug you take
That is making you shake and shiver so?

I was lying after dinner, in my bed, when with a slither
Suddenly, that snake-like Kṛṣṇa bit.
He put his charm upon me, and I'm lucky now you see
To be here to tell my tale and have my wit.

His bite has been so deep that my bady will not sleep.
But Narsī's Lord has had his sport with me
And I'm sure that now my darling won't abandon me.
A starveling,
He will make his home forever now with me.

The dances and love games of Kṛṣṇa and the gopīs are so beautiful that even the angels and heavenly nymphs come down to earth to-watch them.

51

With love she amuses and plays with her lover
Until, when he smiles, she embraces him close.
With rhythm and melody, Kṛṣṇa and the gopīs
Dance with such feeling of enraptured love
That even the heavenly nymphs and musicians
Stand all shame-faced unable to move.

The sages divine and the angels on high
Praise Kṛṣṇa's greatness with words full of joy.
The heavenly nymphs too, have fallen in raptures
At his divine play, which bless'd Narsī beheld.

All the gopīs dress themselves in their finest clothes and ornaments to go and meet Kṛṣṇa. Narsī Mehtā describes this enchanting scene of the gopīs dressed in yellow garments and shining pearls, and compares them with the tidal waves of the sea. All the gopīs have collectively become vāsakasajjā nāyikās (ready to meet their beloved).

52

In Vrindā forest he played his magic flute
And the heart of the gopīs were ensnared.
To each he gave such promises in secret,
That each was enchanted that he cared.

The gopīs prepared themselves to meet the Lord of all,
Made-up and dressed up, they set out together
Looking like the sea in tidal weather.

They were dressed in yellow garments
And wore necklaces of pearl.
With their ankle bells a-jingle, with their side-locks in a curl
The fair gopīs looked so lovely: coloured gems
On their bracelets, pendants, earrings, their lips a tempting red.
Seeing all the gopīs, Hari came to Vrindā's glade.
Narsī is blessed indeed to witness how with them all he played.

Instead of welcoming the gopīs who have come dressed to dance with Kṛṣṇa, he admonishes them for leaving their husbands and children. The gopīs feel rejected and deceived (khaṇḍitā nāyikā). They request him not to torment them as they love Kṛṣṇa alone. Hearing this, Kṛṣṇa accepts them and ends his cruel game.

53

Kṛṣṇa said 'Why have you gopīs all come here to me?
Your conduct is adulterous, and of that I don't approve.
You must go back to your homes and husbands whom you surely love?'

Hearing Mohana's cruel words, the gopīs looked at once downcast
And said 'Oh king of Vrindā, you use words that burn like fire.
Why do you utter now such fearful words ?'

With tearful eyes, the gopīs said, in tones of lamentations,
'Great Murāri, Mohana, if you reject us
Then we shall end our melancholy lives.'

Aware now of the depth of the gopīs' love for him
Hari smiled and was brimful of joy,
Immediately accepting them. The gopīs in this way
Were, with Narsī's Lord, united once again.

Kṛṣṇa's flute enchants Rādhā so much that she forgets all her household chores; and she is punished next day for her neglect. The therefore requests Kṛṣṇa not to play his magical, hypnotic flute.

54

Why do you play on your flute to enchant us
My darling Śyāma? You know very well
The sound of your flute is so very inviting
We cannot resist it. Why alarm us so?

Oh Nanda's son, you are always quite shameless;
You know even at midnight we'll rush to meet you,
Also you know we are blamed next morning—
Why then do you on tempting us so?

My Lord, I implore you in future to think
Before you make gestures inviting us on;
We are women who have little strength to resist you.
Narsī's master, be kind to us, we are your slaves,
All we want is fulfilment of all our desires.

The magical music of Kṛṣṇa's flute gives supreme joy and ecstasy to Rādhā, who forgets all cares of this world and reaches the highest spiritual bliss.

55

Companion mine, last night I heard the music of the flute;
It came from deep in Vrindā woods, it woke me from sleep.
Lost was my heart in that sweet sound, its flawless purity
Led me through waking state, and dream, and even yet beyond.
Past dreamless state my mind went on, beyond all worldly cares.[1]
The qualities of middle, good, and low, I passed all three.[2]
Attachments of all earthly kind were cast out of me.
Wherever I could see the play of Narsī divine Lord,
There would I go with love-filled eyes. My heart if full of joy
For I have seen with my own eyes the greatness of my Lord.

[1]A reference to the Vedānta idea of the states of consciousness: waking (jāgrat), dreaming (svapna), deep sleep (suṣupti), pure intuitional consciousness (turīya) and trance (samādhi or turīyātita).

[2]Three fundamental qualities of nature (prakṛti) according to Sāṅkhya philosophy: good (sattva), middle (rajas) and low (tamas) or intelligence, energy and static inertia.

At the end of the monsoons, all the fields become green with fresh grass. This is the time when the cows have the best grazing. This is also the time for rejoicing and festivals. The cowherds of Vrindavana celebrate the end of the rains with the rāsa dance. This is *the* chance for lovers to meet and come close. The gopīs take this opportunity to dance and sport with Kṛṣṇa. Even the heavens rejoice by showering divine flowers on Kṛṣṇa and the gopīs.

56

Blessed is the beauty of the wooded Vrindāvana
Blessed too this charming month Āso.[1]
Noble is the sound that pours from Kṛṣṇa's magic flute—
And joyously the gopīs dance the rasa.[2]

That inviting women ties a knot in her saree's end, to show
By symbol, the union of the two.
She makes her body wiggle in a most seductive way
And her eyes make captivating movements too.

She then, to her beloved, gives soft words and charming verse
Which she sings in a voice that of the fabled nightingale;
She sings indeed so sweetly that the heavenly choirs pale
And the King of Heaven[3] and all his host come down.

The inhabitants of heaven, looking down on Kṛṣṇa's dance,
Are moved to shout 'Bravo ! Bravo !' in joy.
The gods of all the worlds are there to see this wondrous sight
And Indra's wife makes flowers to shower like rain.

[1]The lunar month of Āśvina (September-October), during the Indian autumn.

[2]The circular folk dance of nothern and western India.

[3]Indra.

Blessed are the gopīs, blest the dance, and the dancer too;
So Narsī too was fortunate to hear,
And beat the rhythmic tempo of this great celestial dance—
Thank the kindness of the gopīs' Lord so dear.

This short song describes how the gopīs are hypnotized by the magic sound of Kṛṣṇa's flute.

57

Hearing Kṛṣṇa's flute at midnight coming from the Vrindā wood,
The gopīs rushed to find him, with no thought of whether they should.
Their passion was so great, that in their haste to join their Lord
They neither bothered to adorn themselves nor cared for in-laws' words,
When they saw Lakṣmī's beloved, their eyes feasted on him there
They rejoiced in Vrindā forest. Narsī's Lord his pleasure shares.

Rādhā has left her family and broken all social ties to be with Kṛṣṇa. He promises to fulfil her desires and they dance together on the most beautiful moonlit night of autumn.

58

With desire, and love's strong longings, my darling came to me.
My mind already was enchanted by his music, piercing deep.
'I have left my children, husband, parents and abandoned family ties
All for you my Mohana'. Hearing, Hari smiled into my eyes
Saying 'Darling, you are high born, and I promise you, and vow
To fulfil all your desires, so come and play the rāsa sport now,
On this full-moon night of Śarad ![1] Thus did Narsī's master say
And that one night seemed six months to them, of sporting and of play.

[1]The full moon night of Autumn (Śarad) is traditionally considered to be the most beautiful moonlit night of the year.

This song describes the rāsa dance of Kṛṣṇa and the gopīs on a calm clear, moonlit night in autumn.

59

In a clearing in Vrindāvana forest, the gopīs
Along with the 'Cowherd' are dancing for sport.
Śyāma plays the flute as he dances, and others
Beat the rhythm on pakha and khanjari too.[1]

The night sky was bright with the full moon of Śarad
That full moon was high in the sky,
The beautiful gopīs, adorned with gold necklets,
Surrounded their master the beloved Govinda.

Their earrings twinkled and sparkled in the moonlight
And their necklets of pearl shone pearly white.
The bells on their ankles made tinkling music,
Their gestures wove patterns around in the air.

Seeing the sport of the blessed one of Devakī,
Heaven's inhabitants, nymphs and gods,
Were so full of joy that they sent down a rain of flowers;
Narsī was there too, with lamp in his hand.

[1] Two types of drum.

This song celebrates the beauty of Kṛṣṇa's physical form and his rāsa sport with the gopīs. Though there was only one Kṛṣṇa and many gopīs, each gopī felt that Kṛṣṇa was dancing with her. The heavens rejoiced, and so did Narsī Mehtā, to see this wonderful sight.

60

Take me, Oh take me to Vrindāvana forest
The voluptuous Cupid I'm longing to see.
Marks of his beauty are sixteen in number
Calm as moonlight, sweet as nectar is he.
His crown has for ornament a peacock's tail feather
And see how the rings in his ears do shine.
He plays on his flute such melodic sweet tunes
Just to hear Hari, girls gather in line.
The girls wear wristbands and earrings gem-studded
From their necks precious pearls hang whose beauty is matchless
Giving much pleasure to everyone's eyes.
The bands at their waists look like lotuses full-blown.
They wear an array of gorgeous gold sarees
Which match the gold of their ankle bells.
Silver toe rings shine, and ankle bells jingle.
But the flute-player's heart is enraptured at last
By the beautiful flowers that they wear in their hair.
In ornaments decked so sensual they looked
That the Dark One began to dance with them all,
When the dance started the ankle bells jingled
With beats of the drum and music from the flute;
In the dance was one Mādhava between every two.
Immortals who blessed them, their foots' dust desired.[1]

[1]i.e. The gods in heaven—Indra, Varuṇa, Kubera etc.—blessed Kṛṣṇa the cowherd and desired the dust from the feet of Kṛṣṇa, the avatāra of Lord Viṣṇu.

Brahmā and the gods uttered words of great pleasure
And showered upon them a light rain of flowers.
Narsī was there too—Umā's husband beside.[2]

[2]Umā's husband is Śiva. This is a reference to Narsī Mehtā's spiritual ecstasy and vision in the temple at Gopnath.

Though the gopīs all live in Gokula, their minds are always in the forest of Vrindavana where Kṛṣṇa plays his enticing flute and where the gopīs run to dance with their beloved Lord. In this song, Narsī Mehtā describes the beauty of the rāsa-līlā dance and invites the gopīs to join the dance.

61

Dance with us the rāsa dance darling,
Prove your forest Vrindāvana
More lovely than Gokula.

You have played enticing music
On your flute, by Jamunā's banks
Your playing so bewitched the gopīs
They've come forgetting their infants' cries.

Gopīs have come to welcome Kṛṣṇa—
In such haste did they prepare
That eye-shadow's in one eye only
And in their ears their toe rings shine.

Having given you, my darling,
Body, mind and soul, they stood
With folded hands in wondrous awe
To see the beauty of your face.

Full moon of Śarad shone through the trees
To make the forest exquisite.
My darling stood in tribhaṅga[1] pose
So handsome in repose.

[1] See foot note on song 82 (14).

Now Narsī says whoever sees
And hears the dance and flute
Of Rādhā-Kṛṣṇa, surely goes
To the highest Vaikuṇṭha heaven.

Rādhā requests her mother not to stop her from going to play and dance with Kṛṣṇa. All her companions have gathered and the dance has already begun. Rādhā wants to go and dance with Kṛṣṇa and has no fear of social disapproval.

62

Please mother do not hold me back
For I love Nanda's son so much !
He inspires love in great god Brahmā
What then of me, a mere woman?

Blessed my friend, dancing with Hari,
Just see how happy she looks now
For she has seen the calm and beauty
Showing in Hari's face.

Mother do not look so angry.
Why prevent my going now
To see my darling Yadunātha?[1]
All my companions are now gathering
Ready to dance with Nanda's son.

I know that people may well gossip
Harbouring evil thoughts of me,
But I don't care, my joy is only
Sporting in love with Narsī's Lord.

[1]The Lord of the Yadu clan: A name of Kṛṣṇa.

The sound of Kṛṣṇa's flute and the full-moon night of autumn are enough to make Rādhā, and the other gopīs, mad with longing for Kṛṣṇa. They all go rushing to meet him.

63

The gopī runs through Vrindā forest
Her lips pour forth 'Kṛṣṇa, Kṛṣṇa.'
She is bewitched by the flute's sweet music
She runs, unmindful of her family's shame.

Śarad's full moon brightens the night,
And autumn's breeze is warm as breath.
The music has her so enraptured
All she desires is Kṛṣṇa's sport.

All the women were so restless,
Made so by the music's power,
Impassioned so, they had forgotten
Even to wear their clothes and gems.

Alone they came out of their houses
Discarding husband, mother, son;
All that they wanted this bright evening
Was to sport with Narsī's Lord.

Once Kṛṣṇa embraced Rādhā. From that day she has fallen madly in love with him and pines for him day and night. This song describes Rādhā's state of mind.

64[1]

How, or when, my darling cast this spell
I do not know, but of one thing I'm sure :
Bewitched I am. Most likely by his flute's sweet words.
His eyes, like two sharp arrows, pierce my heart;
How can you, who are my healer, wound me so ?

You, among sensual people, stand supreme,
Oh Kṛṣṇa, you have charmed my heart with words.
One day, whilst I was dancing rāsa dance
He stepped upon the end of my saree
And enfolded me in his embrace.
From that day on, I have lost all sense
I feel that perhaps I have gone mad.
I've lost all my companions, who once came
To help me carry water from the Jamunā.
Hari's love enkindled in my heart
A flame which makes my eyes flow day and night.
This all began during our midnight sport
Caused by that libertine, that Narsī's Lord.

[1]This is the 25th song in the printed text of the *Śṛṅgāra mālā*. I have not translated the 24th song because it is incomplete.

Though Rādhā is always longing for Kṛṣṇa, sometimes when he is near her, she assumes a posture of pride. Half teasing, and half proud, she refuses his loving advances.

65

No, beloved, you shall not drink
The nectar of my lips.
My handsome one, I know you've come
To palyfully enjoy
The fullness of my breasts, but love
I will not be your toy.

Behaviour such as this, is strange.
My family never had
Before known habits such as this,
They think of it as bad.

Let yogīs great bow down to you
I still have my self pride.
Even such jesting with Narsī's Lord
Carries one through the world's tide.

As a joke, Kṛṣṇa pretends that he is innocent of all the secrets of love play and therefore Rādhā volunteers to teach him.

66

Why my beloved darling don't you come
To embrace me? Why do you close your eyes
When, after separations, I hold you ?

You are Nanda's son, a mere cowherd,
As such, I don't suppose you would know how
The princely arts of love should be performed ?

Hari, if you so say, I shall teach you,
Beloved libertine, how to embrace.
Just follow my instructions carefully:
You press my breasts, and kiss me, and put your arms round here.
When you embrace like this, my love, I'll naturally cry 'No !'
But hold me tight in your embrace; my Lord let me become
As one with you, for without you, the master of Narsī,
I have no chance at all of that sweet union sublime.

This song paints a very delicate picture of love making between Rādhā and Kṛṣṇa.

67

While Śyāma and the young woman were deep in charming talk
She became excited and impassioned from head to toe.
Vanamālī[1] held both her hands, and sometimes put one hand
Upon her heart, and other times he touched her garment's edge.
But looking at her loving eyes which showered him with love,
At once he was his lady's slave, and gentle as a dove.
Blessed is the life of that young girl, who sports 'mid Vrindā's trees,
Blessed are the eyes of Narsī too, for they divine sport see.

[1] 'The one who wears a garland of wild flowers': An epithet of Kṛṣṇa.

In spite of Rādā's love affair with Kṛṣṇa, she sometimes pretends to be innocent and complains to her friends and relatives about Kṛṣṇa's flirtation with her.

68

I shall never go again to the river Jamunā's banks
For on the way I'm sure to meet that Nanda's son—and then
He'll flirt with me in front of all, and never stop.

We are simple Ahir tribal girls, and Kṛṣṇa's a tough man.
Even Nanda cannot stop him and Yaśodā doesn't mind.

He finds all the loneliest places on the Vrindā forest paths
To stop me, where his secret love becomes so very strong
That if I make one sign to him, of welcome, I am his.
This is how, alone, I met Narsī's dear Lord.

Generally Rādhā describes the beauty of Kṛṣṇa. In this unusual song, Kṛṣṇa passionately describes the seductive form of Rādhā.

69

'Your gestures are so precious and your beauty knows no price'
Śyāma says, and then goes on, 'The more I see your face,
The more convinced I am that among women you hold the pride of place.

On your feet are golden bells which make melody as-you walk.
Your nose adorned with sparkling gems, and pearls around your neck;
The flowers in your hair, divine, and Oh ! those ornaments;
I dare not try embracing you, because your firm hard breasts,
If I embrace you tight my love, will surely hurt my chest.'

Her breasts were hard because she wore a tightly laced bodice;
So they stood there, she, Vanamāli in that predicament;
But finally he touched her hand, and to his joy he found
Her body soft as cream and Narsī's master union found.

This last song of the *Śṛngāra mālā* is set in the popular morning melody (prabhātīyā) mode. The sun is about to rise. The sounds of early morning are clearly heard. Rādhā requests Kṛṣṇa to let her go.

70

My love, the moon set long ago and it is daylight now.
How long shall we keep lying here, bound in this tight embrace?
Please my Lord, don't stop me now—the sun is in the east;
The stars look faint, and I hear now the voice of the hungry calf.

Now I can even hear the talk of all the village girls,
And sounds of churning milk are in the air,
The lamps have lost their brightness now and the morning wind
is cool.

The lotuses have opened wide and set the trapped bees free.[1]
Please my beloved, Narsī's Lord, let go and promise me
In future times, at the sun's rise, you'll always set me free.

[1]This refers to a stylized poetic image which is very common in the classical Sanskrit poems (mahā-kāvyas): The bee is so much in love with the lotus that, at night, when the lotus folds its petals, the bee prefers to stay trapped inside all night rather than boring a hole through the petals to escape.

BHAKTI, JÑĀNA ANE VAIRĀGYA NĀ PADO

[71 – 100]

Narsī Mehtā appeals to mankind to remember the holy name of Śrī Hari and to abandon attachment to things that pass away. It is desires that befog man's mind and make him unhappy.

71 (3)

Remember Śrī Hari, let go your attachments,
Think very deeply of your real roots.
Who you are really, and what you're attached to;
Not knowing this, you are shouting 'Mine ! Mine !'

This body is not yours, if you knew the truth of it.
Try as hard as you can you will not keep it long.
This body will go and you'll have many new ones,
With new sons and wives coming row after row.

Always you crave for wealth and desires,
And that keeps you standing apart from the Lord.
He is always close by, but you do not observe him,
Defeating yourself in this great game of life.

You are in deep sleep and are slowly being smothered.
Why don't you awake, hearing words from the saints ?
Awake and your troubles will be over forever.
Narsī will be put to shame if you do not awake.

A life based on desires is like a sand castle: it will soon collapse. When it does, there will be pain and unhappiness. Therefore, let men surrender themselves to Kṛṣṇa and he will lead them to salvation.

72 (4)

Lazy and foolish man, think of Śrī Hari;
End the painful long circle of death and rebirth.
Your petty engagements will not get you anywhere.
Some little joys—then death takes you away.

Salvation lies at the feet of Śrī Kṛṣṇa,
Surrender and you will have eternal joy.
Let go of petty worldly illusions—
Oh remember Śri Kṛṣṇa, remember him always.

As soon as you hear this, discard your attachment,
Stick to the feet of the sweet Lord Śrī Kṛṣṇa.
The palace of worldly desires you are building
Has rotten foundations which will make it fall.

You've lost all your youth and your body is old
And yet you do not think of Kṛṣṇa even now.
Now but a few days are left you to *wake up* !
Let go of the trinket and get heaven's joy.

Those who have surrendered themselves to Śrī Hari
Have all been enlightened, the great sages say;
Poor Narsī says that he loves God intensely,
Worldly life compares ill with a life spent in praising God.

According to the ancient doctrine of karma and punarjanma, a soul is bound to the cycle of life, death and rebirth, through many plant and animal species until it is born as man. As a human being there is now freedom either to seek true knowledge and become free from the cycle, or to be born again. God has helped the soul to be born as a human being. But foolishly man forgets that the creator has given him this golden opportunity to escape from the bondage of birth and death; so Narsī Mehtā exhorts man to surrender to Kṛṣṇa and attain salvation.

73 (5)

Sweet Hari has loved you, yet you have forgotten.
After being a beast he has made you a man.
As an animal you were beaten and pushed around.
Now you're respected as man, why forget Hari's love.

As an oil-presser's bull you were prodded, blind-folded,
Round and round with a yoke on your neck.
Śrī Nātha has saved you, and yet you are selfish
And don't think of his kindness and worship his feet.

By rattling your hooves you once begged for your fodder
And by shaking your head you made signs of your thirst.
And now you've become a man you are ashamed
To dance in the streets singing Govinda's praise.

You once had a long neck to reach the fruit of thorny trees,
As a camel you carried heavy weights on your back.
Now as a man, you eat sweets and roam light and free,
Yet you do not remember sweet Vaikuṇṭha's Lord.

Once your back was pressed down by a heavy gold howdah.
You were pricked with a goad and bent low to be mounted.
Now as man you are covered with perfumes and jewels :
Walking around now as free as the air.

He has given you food, clothes and ornaments even,
When once as a bird you would sing for your seed.
Narsī's Lord has now shown you his grace and compassion
How can you, how can you forget Hari now?

Kṛṣṇa is the supreme Lord. He is the salvation of mankind. Even the gods Brahmā, Śiva and Indra sing his praise.

74 (6)

A man is impure if he doesn't praise Kṛṣṇa,
No matter what number of times he may bathe.
Where Hari's bhakta sings praises to Kṛṣṇa,
You'll find all the places of pilgrimage there.

Kṛṣṇa's supreme above all other men,
He is complete, so to worship elsewhere
Is like tying a bull up and trying to milk it
Instead of Kāmadhenu, the all-giving cow.[1]

Astronomer Garga sang Kṛṣṇa's praises,[2]
Nārada stops not in repeating his name;
Yet the supreme Lord, came to look at the gopī—
Entranced by her love, he stood there by her door.

Brahmā, Śiva and Indra the king of the gods
Have not seen the true Lord, not even in dreams.
The Vedas describe him as 'Not this. Not this'.[3]
Lord Viṣṇu's Śeṣa can't sing all his greatness—
Poor Narsī is trying to sing in his praise.

[1] The wish-fulfilling cow that came up at the churning of the ocean. She belonged to sage Vasiṣṭha.

[2] Garga was the earliest astronomer in India and the chief priest of Kṛṣṇa and the Yādava clan.

[3] This refers to the famous Vedāntic analysis of '*neti, neti*' (not this, not this) progressively negating all names and forms to finally arrive at that which is beyond all names and forms—i.e. the underlying truth, Brahman.

According to the bhakti cult, the only way to salvation in this evil age of Kali yuga is the sincere remembrance of God and a constant repetition of his names. Narsī therefore appeals to mankind not to forget the Lord, but to repeat his name.

75 (7)

Say Hari Hari, for in this dark age
It is the best way if you wish to be saved.
Śyāmasundara depends on his loyal devotees,
He will not forget you—you'll surely be saved.

On your head time is dancing at every moment.
Why do you run after fleeting joys?
In the bat of an eyelid your time will be over—
So of your petty glories, do not be so proud.

Because of great sins your soul keeps returning.
You stand on thin branches not holding the trunk.
The Lord doesn't divide bhaktas—one from another,
It is we in our ignorance, who stand apart.

Let go this illusion—take hold of the truth.
Let your tongue speak the name everlasting.
Narsī asks you to forget not your love for the Lord.
Beside it, all the rest in this world is like dust.

This song stresses the urgency of surrendering to God and seeking salvation. Man is lazy and life is short and full of troubles. Therefore, now is the time to think of the Lord.

76 (8)

What sins have I committed Lord that I feel so sleepy?
I'm lazy and dull—not repeating your name.
My thoughts will not stay on you even a moment,
For thoughts of what gains I may get from you here.

Days pass by and my mind is full of evil.
What with thoughts of the world, I have no time for devotion.
Affairs of the world have just eaten the time up,
My devotion to you has been lost in this way.

This body is fleeting, and karma must end.
You are known as the saviour of people like me.
I just think of you daily again and again
For to purify sinners is your greatest fame.

The pain and anxieties that we all suffer,
Against your pure grace, have no strength at all.
Narsī is crying, he thinks of you always,
So break off his chains—let him come to your feet.

Narsī stresses the necessity of surrounding oneself with the influence of the good, and keeping away from evil. The boy Prahlāda, on account of Nārada's good company, reached salvation, while Rāhu (the ascending nonde of the moon) though immortal became evil in evil company, i.e. in the company of the demonic powers (rākṣasas).

77 (9)

Without company, Lord, of your devotees' servants[1]
My mind plummets, becomes confused.
In evil companionship the mind becomes evil
And an evil mind resists your praise.

With wickedness spread by the evil minded,
The good dies; as poison kills bodies off.
Those people who live lives far off from your goodness
Corrupt and destroy all the good in our hearts.

Ambrosia's power cannot cure all the evils.
Rāhu drank nectar and yet he's still bad.[2]
But the demon Prahlāda was saved by Śrī Kṛṣṇa[3]
Because of his friendship and company of Nārada.

Four ways to salvation,[4] each different from the other,
Yet all are effective in their different ways.
But Narsī with hands folded requests dear Hari
To give him devotion for all time to come.

[1]Satsanga: association with saints is essential for spiritual aspirants.

[2]Rāhu drank nectar during the churning of the ocean by gods and anti-gods.

[3]In his man-lion (Nara-siṃha) incarnation.

[4]This may refer to the traditional four methods of salvation or reintegration (yoga): Haṭha (physical harmony), mantra, laya (merging of the mind) and bhakti (devotion). Or it may refer to the pāñcarātra doctrine of the four vyūhas (emanations) of Kṛṣṇa, as Vāsudeva, Saṅkarṣaṇa, Pradyumna and Aniruddha.

In this song, Narsī Mehtā urges mankind to follow traditional religious laws and to seek enlightenment through them. This follows very closely the advice given by Kṛṣṇa to Arjuna in the *Bhagavad gītā* (III. 35): It is better to do one's duty however devoid of merit it may be, than to do the duty of another. To die doing one's traditional duty is good. The duty of another is always full of danger.

78 (10)

When night's quarter is all that remains,
One who is pious should not be asleep—
But awake and thinking upon the dear Lord,
Repeatedly saying 'there is only you'.

The yogīs should practice their yoga sincerely;
The bhogīs[1] should give up attachment to things;
The rituals of Vedas should be understood;
Vaiṣṇavas' thoughts must stay on their dear Lord.

The poets must think out some inspiring verse;
Those who are charitable, empty their purse;
The wife that's devoted, notes what her spouse says,
Spreading good will at home and wherever she stays.

Understanding deep meaning of each his actions.
Each one should follow the dharma prescribed;
Narsī says, those who remember his master
Will escape being reborn and gain the prize.

[1]Those who are attached to sensual pleasures.

To be born as a human being and not remember the Lord is worse than being born as a beast. Those who shun Kṛṣṇa are a burden on mother earth and their life is wasted.

79 (11)

The one who does not love the dear son of Nanda
Is just like a dog in human form.
He is born to increase the earth's heavy burden,
For love's the great moving force in this world.

The one who does not declare he loves Kṛṣṇa
Is just like a messenger of the god of death.
His sight is pure evil, his joys are futile,
And his words are as heavy as stones.

The one who does not sing the praise of Śrī Kṛṣṇa
Has a mouth that is alwas locked.
Narsī says one who has not known dear Hari
Is encircled by darkness, and blocked.

The sweetest experience in life is love for lord Kṛṣṇa. The name of the Lord is to the devotee like food to a starving animal.

80 (12)

Once having tasted the love of the Lord,
All other things taste too sour.
Just like an animal when it is starving,
It needs grass, not four theories to eat.

Parikṣit knew not the essence of loving,[1]
Śuka did, but he hid its real taste.[2]
He wrote about knowledge and renunciation
And pointed the path to salvation.

God saves even evil ones that he destroys,
There are many wise men, silent men and yogīs,
But the knowers of union and divine love are few;
They stand unique like the gopīs of Vraja.

Love and enlightenment's all that they wanted.
In a way they were selfish, like merchants' desires.
They strongly desired their divine beloved;
They'd been singing his praise over many lives.

I've had the great joy of being held by the hand
By the gopīs' master and Lord,
Now for nothing else can I find any liking;
Narsī sings in great praise of the Lord.

[1] and [2]Śuka was the son of Vyāsa, the arranger and editor of the *Vedas*, author of the epic *Mahābhārata* and most of the early *Purāṇas*. Śuka was born pure and enlightened. Parikṣit was the king of Hastināpura (Delhi area) and the grandson of Arjuna, the famous Pāṇḍava warrior of the *Mahābhārata*. Parikṣit was cursed and was destined to die by snake-bite. Śuka recited the *Bhāgavata Purāṇa*—supreme gospel of devotion—to Parikṣit in the interval, of about eight days, between the curse and his death. Though Śuka knew the gospel of love, he was a jñānī and had no need for it. For Parikṣit, unfortunately, it was too late.

This song relates the story of Viṣṇu's incarnation as the Brahmin dwarf Vāmana. According to this famous Purāṇic legend, Bali was a demonic (i.e. non-Aryan) but charitable ruler. His charity made the gods in heaven jealous. They appealed to Viṣṇu, who, in the form of a dwarf, asked king Bali to give him land no wider that what he could cover in three steps. The king readily agreed, though his priest Śukrācārya tried to dissuade him. The dwarf swelled up to an immense size, covering in two strides the entire univease. The third stride fell on the head of the king and forced him down into the nether regions. As a reward for his magnanimity, Bali was made the ruler of the lowest regions. Narsī uses this story in the song to show how God helps his devotees and those who call upon him for help.

81 (13)

Hari came to the door of king Bali disguised
As a poor Brahmin dwarf singing hymns.
Bali came running right out of his palace
And said ask for whatever you want.

I am seeking a place, sir, to put up my hut.
There are Brahmins around who seek wealth,
They wander around seeking costly gifts
But I do not ask you for all this.

Take whatever you want—ask for palace-like temples,
Why ask just for three steps of land?
Ask for safes full of treasure and these I will give you
And elephants covered in gold.

What use is an elephant to a poor mendicant?
I'm not greedy but just a poor dwarf
Who has taken the vow that for all of my life
I'll not marry but live celibate.

Śukra warned Bali—this dwarf's really Viṣṇu,
But Bali felt proud that the Lord

Had come to his house and was begging for alms.
A philanthropists' dream—what a chance !

While Bali poured water to seal up his promise,
Śukra, as insect, crawled into the spout.
In anger king Bali then poked out the insect
And knocked one of Śukra's eyes out.

Poor Bali was crushed to the ground by the Lord
This was done as a favour to Indra.
Narsī says Hari in so many like ways
Is always helping his devotees.

This song describes the form of Kṛṣṇa in great detail and Narsī Mehtā then urges the devotee to meditate on this form.

82 (14)

On beloved of Nanda do your meditation.
Bliss everlasting will be your reward.
All the eight powers will wait at your doorstep[1]
And the karmas will all be destroyed.

He wears Peacock feathers—on him put your thoughts.
His ear-rings are the shape of makaras.[2]
The mark on his forehead's of pure yellow saffron
Round his neck there's a necklace of pearls.

The cloth round his waist is also of yellow,
He stands in tribhaṅga[3] with his flute.
So restful his pose beneath the kadamba tree,
With Rādhikā singing close by.

Mad with love, upon hearing the sound of his flute,
The women come running to him.
They shower him with garlands of flowers and pearls
And Narsī is overjoyed.

[1]Eight yogic and miraculous powers are: the power to become like an atom (aṇimā), light as wool (laghimā), very heavy (garimā), and limitless (mahimā); to have strong will power (prākāmya), control over mind and body (iśitva), over natural elements (vaśitva) and over desires (kāmāvasāyitva).

[2]Mythical sea monster which has the body of a fish and the head of an antelope or lion. The shape of this monster is used as a decorative motif in Indian art.

[3]Tribhaṅga: literally means 'three bends' and refers to triple bend or S-shaped posture of the body used in Indian dance and iconography.

Unless mankind awakens from the long sleep of ignorance, and surrenders to God, there is no hope of salvation. And without salvation, man will have to go through, again and again, the painful cycle of birth and death.

83 (15)

How can you sleep? Remember Lord Hari,
Without him none can save you.
The crowds of relations, mother, father and sons—
When death comes they will all run away.

You probably hung upside-down and did *tapas*
To merit being born as a man.
But now born as man, you are tied to illusions,
Surrounded by meanness and greed.

Day and night while you're waking, and in your sleep too,
Dreaming as well—illusions fill you.
By chance you have now got the prized human birth
But not a moment to think of Śrī Hari.

You are now hypnotized by thoughts of wealth,
The pain of rebirth is forgotten
In the womb it was He who cared for you.

Enough now, enough—you have had enough pain,
Stir yourself now and awake:
How many times do you want to be told
Narsī's master removes all your pain.

Narsī Mehtā calls upon mankind to remember Kṛṣṇa again and again. There is no other way to salvation.

84 (16)

Saints truly adore the feet of Govinda.
Human bodies are just made of dross.
Sing Kṛṣṇa, Kṛṣṇa again and again,
You'll get joy just repeating his name.

The gods in their heavens want to worship Lord Hari
While silly man just forgets.
I swear Kṛṣṇa's name is the only real way,
Let your heart never leave it at all.

The great yogīs and saints roam in the forests
To get just a glimpse of the Lord.
And Lord Viṭṭhala just goes to graze cows like a cowherd.
Narsī says think of him and be saved.

This song is based on the ancient Indian doctrine of the inflexible law of karma which declares that 'as a man sows, so shall he reap'. But man in his foolishness sows bitter seeds and expects sweet results. According to Narsī, the only way out of this prison of karma is either to surrender to God or to become selfless.

85 (17)

All you men, you are proud—but of what?
Of this body which one day must rot?
But consider your actions—you plant bitter seeds
And expect to eat pulses and wheat.

Charity? You will not give a goat.
But you expect to be given fine cows.
It's like giving a goldsmith some brass
Expecting gold ornaments back.

Good deeds bring prosperity and joy
And by giving you get in return;
So Narsī says 'give' of your best to the Lord,
In return you'll inherit the earth.

In this beautiful song Narsī gives symbolic meaning to Kṛṣṇa, his family and all those who surround him in Gokula, Mathura and Dvaraka.

86 (18)

Blessed is Yaśodā that the Lord is her son,
God himself came to give Nanda joy,
And the Lord's not alone, he brought serpent Śeṣa
Who has come as his brother Balarāma.

The gods of the heaven have become the gopālas.
Lakṣmī's become the gopīs.
The wives of great sages have become trees and creepers.
Devotion has appeared in Rādhā's form.
The foster mother of Kṛṣṇa is really salvation.
Viṣṇu's heaven is now Vraja on earth.

Vasudeva's the Vedas, Vedic meters are cows,
Devakī is knowledge in living form.
Lord Brahmā's his stick and Śiva the flute,
Mahādeva's five heads[1] are the notes thereof.

Indra the king of the gods is Arjuna,
Ahaṃkāra[2] is Duryodhana.
Dharma is Yudhiṣṭhira, all gods are on earth.
Narsī's the devotees' servant.

[1]As the ruler of the five elements and five senses, Śiva is known as five-faced (Pañcānana): Īśāna (ruler), Tat-puruṣa (supreme man), Aghora (nonfearful), Vāma-deva (left-hand-deity) and Sadyojāta (suddenly born).

[2]Ego, pride and the sense of 'I-ness'.

This is a song of surrender. Having wholly surrendered to Him, the poet requests the Lord to give him true devotion, love and salvation. The devotee is a humble nobody whose only chance in life is the grace of God.

87 (19)

Give me devotion to you Lord, forever.
Being poor I rely upon you for my care.
First, Oh my Lord, please give me devotion,
Then come into my heart and live there always.

Having devotion for you, I care naught for the body.
I care not at all for the worldly delights.
If I let go of you, Oh my beloved,
Who will be there then to be my saviour?

I have filled the four walls of my house with much evil.
Now Narsī has only one way to escape,
That is, through the window of dear Kṛṣṇa's name.
Without that life's a dice game without any dice.

Already I've passed through Oh! so many births.
I've been restless without you my Lord.
If I drown in this deep sea of worldliness now,
Excepts you my Lord, who'll pull me out?

Man makes many plans in this very short life—
'I shall do that tomorrow, today I did this.'
But who can be sure we here tomorrow?
Life may end, and our plans, anytime.

You're the first word and the last Oh Viṭṭhala.
Will you not manifest yourself to me?
Poor Narsī is asking to get just a glimpse of you
Oh Lord, show your grace and save me.

Bhakti is the highest and the best path to God. Goods deeds may lead to heaven, but that is still within the cycle of birth and death. Even immortals are bound by the laws of action-reaction (karma). Only the enlightened ones are free from this cycle. And devotion is the most direct path to enlightenment. At the end of the song, Narsī says that only a few have known true bhakti, and among those few are Śiva, Śuka and the gopīs of Vraja.

88 (20)

Adoration for God is the greatest of gifts,
Unknown in the world of great Brahmā.
Good action will take one to the immortals' heaven
But even that only after eighty four births![1]

True devotees of Hari don't crave final salvation,
They ask to be born many times
To serve the son of Nanda and sing praises of him,
Celebrating his greatness and his form.

Those who've been born in this country of Bharata
And have praised Lord Govinda, are bless'd.
Bless'd are their family, mother and father
And bless'd is their true human birth.

Bless'd is Vrindāvana and the people of Vraja;
The eight great perfections are theirs,
To wait upon them; and their maid
Is salvation, who takes care of them.

The divine flavours' taste is known to Śiva and Śuka,
The gopīs of Vraja know it too.
But Narsī says that if he's put by their side
He will look like a real hedonist.

[1]The eighty-four births are the different animal and plant forms that a soul is supposed to pass through before being born a man. And then, if he does good deeds as a man, he is born in the heaven of the immortals (amaraloka).

Narsī extols the merit of the company of holy men who are true devotees of God. They can save the soul from becoming stuck in the mire of worldliness.

89 (21)

With the dust from your devotees' feet on my head
I feel I have become blessed.
I see that their love which is like ambrosia,
In an instant, destroys all my sins.

Devotees destory all the dirt of the heart,
As darkness is destroyed by light.
Blessed are those who have the company of saints.
Singing Kṛṣṇa's praise one can see him.

The moment that's spent in the company of saints,
Is the greatest in any man's life.
Narsī says he is sure, for one drowning in sin,
The saints are the only safe boats.

Even though this, and the following song [91 (23)] are included in an anthology of devotional and philosophical songs, they are actually autobiographical. They have been translated here because they represent Narsī Mehtā's most liberal and revolutionary views about the evils of the caste system and the ostracism he had to face on account of his views and actions. They also show Narsī Mehtā to be a sincere and true bhakta.

90 (22)

The lake Dāmodara, at the Girnar hills' foot
Is where Mehtājī bathed every day.
Untouchables were the sincerest devotees,
With hands folded they fell to his feet.

Again and again they requested him humbly—
Please come to our houses to sing;
For your holy songs will spread love and devotion
That will finally free us from rebirth.

Seeing them standing there begging this favour,
Compassion and kindness I felt,
Where distinction is made between one and another,
There is no holiness there.

To the dispassionate mind all beings are one.
I told them to go and prepare
A clear space in their courtyard, and make it look nice.
And that evening Mehtājī went there.

He brought with him food which he offered to God,
Celebrating there all through the night,
Singing and dancing in praise of his Lord.
All who gathered there were overjoyed.

He returned to his house still singing God's name,
With the playing of drums and blowing of conch shells.

The Nāgaras laughed at him and jeered,
Saying 'Is this how a Brahmin behaves?'

Mehtājī remained silent—for what could he say
To minds that were so immature?
Many women and men of the town came to ask him
Why he went against custom like this.

You do not consider your caste or sub-caste,
Nor do you think of society.
To these questions, Narsī says with folded hands.
I love all devotees of Hari.[1]

[1]In this song, Narsī refers to himself in the third person.

See notes on the previous song 90 (22).

91 (23)

I am what you say that I am, if it please you
To think that I am such a one.
If you think I'm not fit to sing Kṛṣṇa's praise,
Then Dāmodara's servant I'll become.

The mind takes upon it the surrounding colour—
My mind was first passionate red,
But now that it's tasted the nectar of Hari
If only can sing in his praise.

Of all in society, I am the lowest.
Lower than the lowest of low.
You may call me by any bad names that you like,
All I know is I'm deeply in love.

I don't understand talk of karma and dharma.
All these things are not near my God.
All who feel higher than these Harijanas[1]
Have wasted there whole human life.

[1] This word means both devotees of Hari and the lower castes of society.

The real power that animates the universe is that of God, but on account of ignorance and ego, man thinks that he is in charge. The seasons change and the trees bear fruits and flowers because of God's will. Mankind is powerless in the face of the laws of nature. The only salvation for man is to surrender to the supreme Godhead.

92 (1)

Whatever the Lord of the universe likes, comes to pass.
What point then in crying over it?
All's in His hands, our will doesn't count.
For salvation call upon him for help.

I am the doer and I am the lord,
Such thinking is pure ignorance.
It's like the dog's that walks under the cart
Thinking he bears the weight of the load.

The whole universe is directed by Him
As yogīs and the great Śiva know.
If it were our fate to order things here,
Then unhappiness no one would show.

They'd kill all their enemies, letting friends live.
There would then be no rich and no poor.
All would then say that they claim to be king,
And the whole of existence is theirs.

The seasons, the trees, the fruits, the leaves are one whole.
But man's foolish mind remains foolishly scattered.
What is due to each person, that person gets.

But people make theories and philosophies
To suit their own selfish ideas.

Actions and words then follow that course
Presuming that they are the truth.

But understand now that the joys of this world
Are ephemeral—without God—unripe.
With folded hands Narsī requests of his Lord—
Give me love of you—birth after birth.

This song refers to the philosophical ideas of Viṣṇusvāmin, and his follower Vallabhācārya. According to these philosophers, the Primeval Soul or the Highest Being felt alone and so created this entire universe out of Himself. Since the universe sprang from the Highest Being, it forms a living part of the Divine and therefore is not an illusion (māyā). The Highest Being is identified with Kṛṣṇa. Narsī Mehtā elaborates this idea by stressing the identity of the animate and the inanimate world with God in the form of Śrī Hari. At the end of the song, he says that just as golden ornaments share the underlying quality of their material cause, gold, so the universe shares the basic quality of the Supreme Being.

93 (2)

In this entire universe, you're the only reality,
But your forms seem many, Oh, Hari !
In the body you're soul, in the sun you are brightness,
The Vedas say you are space, sound.[1]

You are the winds and the waters, and the earth,
The mountains, the trees, the whole cosmos.
These forms were created for your enjoyment,
That's why Śiva and soul are now two.

The Vedas and other texts sny there's no difference
Between gold and golden ornaments.
Only the name and the form appear changed,
The essence of gold is the same.

You're the seed in the tree and the tree in the seed,
The difference is only in the 'looking'.[2]
Narsī says all this is only the mind's own creation,
But I know love and am sure he'll appear.

[1]Sound here refers to the mystical syllable OM-*śabda brahman*—which represents the ultimate sound without attributes and is a symbol of the union of the individual soul (ātman) with the Universal Soul (brahman).

[2]i.e. point of view—the way one looks at reality.

Without surrender and love, true knowledge cannot be attained. Scholarly study does not help at all. Books and philosophical systems are a web of empty words and no more. They cannot lead to enlightenment. In fact they only increase false pride and take one away from God. To run after books and scholars is like throwing away rice and eating the husks instead.

94 (3)

Without cleansing yourself you will not know the truth,
The scholars can't get it from books.
Searching for truth in books is just like
Throwing grain away and eating husks.

In enjoying this world all become suffocated,
Without the guru's guidance all go astray.
They get caught in word-games, and so in this way
They throw good clothes away and wear rags.

They learn words and philosophies, quote from all texts,
But they live in worldly illusion.
They do not let go of the worldly ego
And therefore they wander forever.

They talk about the scriptures, but remain in the dark.
In the dark night of ignorance they wander;
Narsī says he has composed all these songs
To understand that which is the truth.

Generally Narsī follows the philosophy of Viṣṇusvāmin, but in this song he refers to the world as an illusion (māyā) that only seems to be real in dreams, but disappears when one awakens. Perhaps Narsī did not follow any set school of thought but found inspiration for his beliefs in the *Upaniṣads* were the proto-types of all later schools of Vedānta are to be found.

95 (4)

When I awaken and look I see there's no world.
But in sleep I see objects of pleasure.
The play of the mind and the consciousness,
Are two absolutes dancing together.

The five elements all from the absolute came.
And they make all the universal atoms.[1]
Just as on the tree, the flowers and the fruit
Are not separate from the roots and the trunk.

The Vedas and other texts say there's no difference
Between gold and golden ornaments.
Only the name and the form appear changed,
The essence of gold is the same.

Soul and Śiva divided because of desire,
And from them have come all the worlds.
Narsī says you are that, you are that: think on this truth
And like the saints of the past you'll be saved.

[1]The elements—earth, water, fire, and air—exist in two forms: transient and eternal. As eternal substances they are in the form of atoms (paramāṇus).

Man usually leaves spiritual matters to a time of life when he has retired from active life and has nothing else to do to fill the time. But Narsī says that by then it is too late. The body has become weak and infirm, and there is no more energy left for the search for enlightenment. The time to start is *now*, when there is still some youth and energy left.

96 (5)

In your youth you forgot to remember Lord Hari.
Your mind was full of worldly things.
You wanted to taste the joys of the five senses
And desired to amass wealth.

Until you were fifty you played in the world,
Then at sixty there came the troubles.
Only at seventy, you understood,
Now you want to retire and gain grace.

You can't see well, your throat is choked with phlegm.
Your voice can now scarcely be heard.
You're still quite attached and you desires are still fresh,
Still you don't see your Refuge.[1]

You can no longer walk without a stick's aid,
Your body is ravaged by age.
There's not a single tooth left in your mouth
And yet your stomach still craves food.

Those who've made the best use of the chance they
 were given[2]
And who've joined with Lord Hari, are bless'd.
Narsī says those who remember God when young and happy
Are blessed and lucky indeed.

[1]i.e. the Lord Śrī Kṛṣṇa.
[2]To be born as human beings.

Narsī is convinced that the only worthwhile spiritual activity is to try and know the 'inner self'. All other ways, like rituals, austerities, study of the scriptures, etc., are a waste of time and merely ways of 'filling the stomach' (i.e. making a living).

97 (6)

If you have not known your real inner self
All yoga and sādhanā are useless.
Your human birth has been a waste,
Like the rain that out of season falls.

What if you've done all your ritual pūjās?
What if you've given alms?
What if you've a jaṭā and and an ash-besmeared body?
What if your hair's all pulled out?[1]

What of asceticism, what of your jātrās?
What if you've done lacs of japa?
What if you've marked your whole body with symbols?
Worn tulasī, drunk Gaṅgā's streams?

What if you've studied the *Vedas* and grammar?
Music and six darśanas?[2]
What if you've observed the strict caste distinctions?
What if you have done all these?

These are games played to fill empty stomachs;
They do not show inner spirit.
Narsī says if you do'nt realise the true self,
You've wasted this gem of a birth.

[1]Hair-plucking: a practice common among Jain monks.

[2]From the Sanskrit root *dṛś*='viewing', 'looking', 'seeing'. Here it refers to the views of the six systems of orthodox Hindu thought: Nyāya-Vaiśeṣika (logic), Sāṁkhya-Yoga (knowledge and practice), Mīmāṁsā (ritual) and Vedānta (metaphysics).

Happiness and misery are natural. They come and go at God's will. Narsī Mehtā then enumerates many great kings, gods and mortals who had to suffer unhappiness and deprivation, even though they were virtuous and pure. But eventually all devotees of God are saved by His grace.

98 (7)

Do not let joy or pain disturb your mind.
You are created by He who is Lord,
The ruler of all of the great Raghu clan.
So be assured—no one can destory you.

Nala was a very grert man,
His queen was called Damayantī,
But she had to roam the forest, naked,
Searching for food and drink.[1]

Think of the five Pāṇḍava brothers,
And their wife who was called Draupadī.
For twelve years they had to stay in the dark forest,
And wander without rest.[2]

Sītā the most faithful wife of Śrī Rāma
Was kidnapped and taken away
By the Śrīlankā demon, the king Rāvaṇa.
And there she faced many hard days.

Or take king Rāvaṇa and his queen Mandodarī.
Though he had the intellect of ten heads,
All his heads were eventually smashed
And his Laṅkā lay ravaged and sacked.

[1]The story of Nala, the king of Niṣadha, and his wife Damayantī is told in the *Mahābhārata*. Nala was ruined in a game of dice.

[2]Descendants of Pāṇḍu. The five heros of the *Mahābhārata*.

Hariścandra was honest, had a beautiful wife.
Her name was Tārāmatī.
When misfortune struck them, she was forced to work
In the house of a most evil man.[3]

Think on all these that have gone before,
Oh! devotees of Hari, remember,
Remember His name and to call upon Him
And you will surely be helped.

Even the gods when they were in trouble
Called upon one who's within,
And when they that, they always found help.
Narsī Mehtā's Lord saved them all.

[3]Hariścandra's wife was also called Śaibyā. She was sold to an evil, old Brahmin of Varanasi to pay the Royal Consecration to Viśvāmitra. His tale is related in the *Purāṇas* and the *Mahābhārata*.

Here again, Narsī Mehtā describes the universe as a living manifestation of the Divine Being Kṛṣṇa. The omnipresent Lord has become everything. He pervades the cosmos and He is the supreme enjoyer of it. The only way man can share in the joy of the 'Supreme Being' is through loving devotion.

99 (8)

Look deep as you can into this vastness of space.
Who pervades it saying 'I'm He'?[1]
There is no one here who is like Lord Kṛṣṇa,
I want to end my life at his feet.

The splendour of the dark one the mind can't comprehend.
I've forgotten all paths id my joy.[2]
All are one—the living and inanimate too,
I've held on to the medicine of love.

In its burning brightness His glory is seen,
A million suns framed in gold light.
It is there that one sees that the eternal plays,
Swinging in a cradle of gold.

Without any cotton or oil or wick,
His pure flame shines forever.[3]
Without using your eyes, you can see His pure form[4]
And taste it without the use of your tongue.

[1]This is one of the mahāvākyas (great sentence from the *Bṛhadāraṇyaka Upaniṣad* stating 'Aham brahmāsmi' (I am Brahman), This expresses the highest Vedāntic truth of the identity of the soul and the Divine.

[2]Paths (panthas) : Narsī Mehtā refers either to the various sects of Hinduism during his time, or to methods of spiritual discipline (sādhanā). In short, he tries to convey the idea that in his love for Kṛṣṇa, he has thrown away all the formalities of sects and disciplines.

[3]Narsī regards the sun to be the most visible power of God.

[4]With the inner eye, the eye of knowledge.

He is everlasting and unknowable,
Beyond all the organs of sense.
Narsī's master pervades everywhere—and beyond,
But saints catch Him in the net of love.

This is perhaps the most popular and widely known song of Narsī Mehtā. It was Mahatma Gandhi's favourite song and was frequently sung during prayer meetings in his ashrama. In this song, Narsī describes, in living detail, the nature of a true and sincere Vaiṣṇava—devotee of God.

100

A true Vaiṣṇava has compassion for all,
Any who suffer he helps,
But having helped he never then feels,
Proud of the deed he has done.

He will bow down his head and make himself low
To all, he despises none.
He is pure in his thoughts, in his speech and his deeds.
Their mothers are blessed by such ones.

His mind is beyond all desires and all passion,
He looks at all women as Mā.[1]
He is not given to telling lies,
Of others he's not envious.

Ignorance will never rule over him,
And his mind is always detached.
In him one can see the Gods' ecstasy.
He is the true 'pilgrimage'.[2]

He knows greed and won't commit fraud,
He has gone beyond desire and anger.
Narsī says it is like freeing all of one's line[3]
To set your eyes on such a man.

[1]i.e. mother.

[2]The original Gujarati is 'sekal tiratha tenā tana mā re' which means that the body of a true Vaiṣṇava is the centre of pilgrimage.

[3]i.e. ancestors.

BIBLIOGRAPHY

Biographical Works

Desai, Icchārām Sūryarām (ed.), *Bṛhat Kāvya Dohan* (*BKD*), parts 1-8, Bombay, 1913 (Guj.).

(i) Ādhār Bhaṭṭ, *Śāmaḷśā no vivāh*, *BKD*, part 8, pp. 418 ff.

(ii) Mūḷjī Bhaṭṭ, *Narsiṁh Mehtānā Pitānun śrādh*, *BKD*, part 8, pp. 484 ff.

(iii) Viśvānath Jāni, *Narsiṁh Mehtānun carit*, *BKD*, part 8, pp. 609 ff.

Munshi, K.M., *Narsaiyo Bhakta Harino*, Bombay, 1952 (Guj.).

———., *Narasiṁh yuganā kavio*, Bombay, 1962 (Guj.).

Nābhājī, *Bhakta māla*, with a commentary by priyādās and another commentary styled *Bhakti-sudhā-bindu-svāda* by Sītārāmśaraṇ Bhagavān prasād, 6 parts, Varanasi, 1903-1909 (Hi.).

Pandya, Gajendrashankar Lalshankar, *Narasiṁh Mehtā*, (R.B. Kalāśankar Pratāpasiṁh Vyākhyān mālā, No. 2) Surat, 1929 (Guj.).

Pratāpasiṁha, *Bhakta māla* of Nābhājī paraphrased as *Bhakti kalpadruma*, edited by Kālicaraṇ Caurasiyā Gauḍ, Lucknow, 1952 (Hi.)

Shastri, K.K. (ed.), *Narasiṁh Mehtā kṛt Ātmacaritnā kāvyo*, Junagadh, 1964 (Guj.).

———. (ed.), *Narsai Mehtānā Pado*, Ahmedabad, 1965 (Guj.).

Vaishnav, Bapubhai Jadavrai (ed.), *Nṛsiṁh Mehtā nā Jīvananā Samarṇo*, Junagadh, 1964 (Guj.).

Historical Background (in Gujarati)

Desai, Śambhuprasād Harprasād, *Saurāṣṭrano Itihāsa*, Junagadh, 1968 (new edition).

Shastri, D.K., *Vaiṣṇava-dharmano Sankṣipta Itihāsa*, (Forbes Gujarati Sabhā Granthāvalī, No. 30), Bombay, 1939 (second edition).

Works in English

Archer, W.G., *The Loves of Krishna, in Indian Painting and Poetry*, London, 1957.

Bhandarkar, R.G., 'Vaiṣṇavism, Śaivism and Minor Religious Systems', in *Encyclopedia of Indo-Aryan Research*, Vol. III, part 6), Strassburg, 1913.

Carpenter, J.E., *Theism in Medieval India*, (Hibbert Lecture—Second Series), London, 1921.

Coomaraswamy, A.K., 'The Eight Nayikas', *Journal of Indian Arts and Industry*, (n.s.) Vol. XVI, 1914, No. 128, pp. 99-112, (8 plates).

Danielou, Alain, *Hindu Polytheism*, London, 1963.

Dimock Jr., Edward C., *The Place of the Hidden Moon—Erotic Mysticism in the Vaishnava-Sahajiya Cult of Bengal*, Chicago, 1966.

Divetia, N.B., *Gujarati Language and Literature*, Vols. I and II, (Wilson Philological Lectures, University of Bombay), Bombay, 1921 and 1932.

Dawson, John, *A Classical Dictionary of Hindu Mythology and Religion, Geography, History and Literature*, London, 1957 (nineth edition).

Farquhar, J.N., *An Outline of the Religious Literature of India*, Varanasi, 1967 (Indian reprint).

Grierson, George A., The Modern Vernacular Literature of Hindustan, printed as a special number of the *Journal of the Asiatic Society of Bengal*, part I, for 1888, Calcutta, 1889.

Isacco, Enrico, et al., (eds.), *Krishna: The Divine Lover—Myth and Legend through Indian Art*, Lausanne, 1982.

Majumdar, M.R., *Cultural History of Gujarat* (*from Early Times to Pre-British Period*) Bombay, 1965.

Majumdar, A.K., *Bhakti Renaissance*, Bombay, 1965.

Mukerjee, Radhakamal, *The Lord of the Autumn Moons*, Bombay, 1957.

Munshi, K.M., *Gujarat and Its Literature: from Early Times to* 1852, Bombay, 1967.

Randhawa, M.S., *Kangra Paintings of Love*, New Delhi, 1962.

Singer, Milton (ed.), *Krishna: Myths, Rites, and Attitudes*, Honolulu, 1966.

Walker, Benjamin, *Hindu World*, Vols. 1 and 2, London, 1968.

Underhill, Evelyn, *Mysticism*, London, 1967,

INDEX

Ahaṃkāra, 122
Ahir, 100
alms, 135
Āḷvārs, 2, 26
Arjuna, 113, 115, 122
āso (month), 85
Āśvina (month), 85
Ātman, 131
ātma-nivedana (surrender), 2, 11
atoms, 133
autobiographical works, 4, 12-13
avatāra, 90

Balabhadra, 26
Balarāma, 14, 26, 122
Bali, 116
Bansidhar, 5
Bhagavadgītā, 1, 15, 113
Bhāgavatapurāṇa, 1, 2, 5, 6, 12, 15, 47
bhakta, 53, 77, 109
bhaktas, 37, 110
bhakti, 1, 2-3, 25, 30, 110, 124
Bhaktisūtras, 1
Bharata, 124
Bhīmā (river), 54
bhogīs, 113
Brahmā, 29, 31, 37, 44, 52, 91, 109, 122, 124
Brahman, 109, 131
Brahmin, 116

cātaka, 46, 58, 59
caste, 127, 135
Chāndogya upaniṣad, 15
collyrium, 62
cowherd, 38, 89
Cupid, 27, 57, 58, 73, 90

Damayantī, 136
Dāmodara, 126, 128
Dark One, 40, 47, 51, 56, 70
Darśanas, 135
Dayākor, 4
Devakī, 14, 122
Dharma, 122
discipline, 25
Draupadī, 136
Duryodhana, 122
Dvaraka, 122

ecstasy, 30, 40, 140

flute, 39, 52, 83, 87, 92, 93, 95, 118, 122

Gandhi, M., 140
Gangā, 135
Garga, 109
Giridhara, 26, 42
Giridhāri, 39
Girnar (hills), 9, 126
Gīta-Govinda, 12, 13, 34
gokula, 39, 46, 122
gopālas, 122
gopikā gīta, 47
gopī(s), 26, 31, 38, 41, 42, 43, 46, 47, 51, 55, 56, 59, 61, 69, 74, 78, 80, 81, 82, 85, 86, 87, 89, 90, 92, 95, 109, 115, 122, 124
Gopnath, 6, 91
Govinda, 46, 89, 107, 120, 124
Govinda gamana, 12, 15, 17
grace, 2
Guru, 132

Hari, 47, 52, 65, 82, 94, 96, 98, 105, 106, 109, 112, 119, 120, 127, 131, 134, 137
Harijana, 128

Hariścandra, 137
Hār mālā, 4, 10-11, 13
holi, 61

Immortals, 25
Indra, 26, 52, 85, 90, 117, 122
intoxicated, 31

Jainism, 1
Jamunā (*also see* Yamunā), 43, 47, 51, 56, 59, 92, 96, 100
japa, 135
jaṭā, 135
Jātrās, 135
Jayadeva, 34, 37
Jñāni, 115

kadamba tree, 74
Kalahāntaritā nāyikā, 73, 75
kali yuga, 110
Kāmadhenu, 109
Kaṃsa, 14, 15
karma, 107, 111, 118, 121, 124
Kān, 63
Khaṇḍitā, 76
Khaṇḍitā nāyikā, 58, 69, 82
kokilā, 34
Kṛṣṇa, 1, 3, 6, 7, 8, 9, 11-17, 25, 26, 27, 28, 29, 30, 31, 32, 33, 34, 35, 36, 37, 38, 39, 40, 41, 42, 43, 45, 46, 47, 49, 50, 51, 52, 53, 54, 55, 56, 57, 58, 59, 60, 61, 62, 63, 64, 65, 69, 70, 71, 72, 73, 74, 75, 76, 77, 79, 80, 81, 82, 83, 84, 85, 87, 88, 89, 90, 92, 93, 94, 95, 96, 97, 98, 99, 100, 101, 102, 106, 107, 109, 112, 113, 114, 115, 118, 120, 122, 123, 125, 128, 131, 138
Kṛṣṇadās, 4
Kubera, 90
kumkum, 41
Kunvarbāi, 8-9
Kunvarbāinun Māmerun, 4, 8, 13

Lakṣmī, 29, 34, 46, 87, 122
Lāl kavi, 18

Mādhava, 59, 90
Madhva, 1
Mahābhārata, 15, 37, 115, 136, 137
Mahādeva, 122
Mahākāvya, 102
Mahāvākya, 138
Mahmud Begḍā, 11-12
makara, 118
Malhāra (rāga), 59
māli, 33
Mandodarī, 136
Mānekbāi, 5, 8
Mathura, 37, 42, 122
māyā, 11, 131, 133
Mehtā, Narsī, 37, 38, 90, 105, 107, 113, 120, 126, 130, 135, 136, 137
Mohana, 51, 69, 82, 88
mother-in-law, 40
Murāri, 52, 82

Nābhājī, 4
Nāgar Brahmin caste, 3, 10, 12
Nāgars, 127
Nala, 136
nanad (sister-in-law), 36, 37
Nanda, 26, 38, 42, 47, 48, 77, 118, 122, 124
Nārada, 1, 14, 37, 77, 109, 112
Narahari, 61
Narasimha, 112
Nāyaṇārs, 2
nāyikās, 16-17, 19
Nimbārka, 1

Omniscient, 52

Pañcama, 55
Pāñcarātra, 112
Pandharpur, 54
Pāṇḍava, 115, 136
Pāṇḍu, 136
Parakiyā nāyikā, 34

Parikṣit, 115
penance, 25
Parvatdās, 4, 5, 19
Phalguṇa (month), 61
pilgrimage, 140
Prabhātīyā, 18, 102
Prahlāda, 112
Premānand, 4, 10, 18
pūjā, 135
punarjanma, 107
Purāṇas, 37, 46, 115, 137
Puṣṭi mārga, 46

Rādhā, 6, 18, 11, 14-17, 19, 25, 26, 27, 28, 30, 31, 32, 33, 34, 35, 36, 37, 38, 40, 41, 44, 45, 46, 49, 50, 52, 53, 54, 56, 57, 58, 59, 60, 62, 63, 64, 65, 69, 70, 71, 72, 73, 74, 75, 76, 77, 79, 83, 84, 88, 93, 94, 96, 97, 98, 99, 100, 101, 102, 122
Rādhikā, 118
Rāga, 55
Raghu, 136
Rāhu, 112
rākṣasa, 112
Rāma, 3, 136
Rā Māṇḍlik, 8, 10, 12
Rāmāyaṇa, 3
Rāsa (dance), 85, 96
Rāsa-līlā, 6, 7, 13, 92
Rāvaṇa, 3, 136

sacred texts, 25
sādhanā, 135, 136
sādhu, 60
Śaibyā, 137
salvation, 26, 106, 107, 110, 119, 120, 122, 124, 129
Śāmalśā, 8
Śāmalśā no vivāh, 4, 13
Sanakādi, 37, 77
Sanada, 37
Śāṇḍilya, 1
Śaṅkara, 11
Sānkhya, 84
Śarada, 88, 89, 92, 95
Sārangapāṇi, 44
satsanga, 112
Śeṣa, 25, 109, 122
sister-in-law, 30, 40, 50, 60, 77
Sītā, 136
Śiva, 91, 109, 122, 124, 129, 131, 133,
soul, 78, 131, 133
Śrīlanka, 136
Śuka, 37, 115, 124
Śukra, 116
Śukrācārya, 116
Surat Sangrām, 17
śvādhinapatikā nāyikā, 69, 72
Śyāma, 63, 73, 83, 89, 99, 101
Śyāmasundara, 110

Talaja, 4, 6
tapas, 119
Tārāmatī, 137
tribhanga, 92, 118
tulasī, 135

Umā, 91
Upaniṣads, 3, 133, 138

Vallabhācārya, 1, 16, 18, 46, 78, 131
vaikuṇṭha, 44, 46, 93, 107
Vaiṣṇavas, 64, 113, 140
Vāmana, 116
Vanamālī, 33, 99, 101
Varanasi, 137
Varuṇa, 90
Vāsakasajjā nāyikā, 71, 81
Vasiṣṭha, 109
Vasudeva, 14, 122
Vedānta, 26, 84, 133
vedāntic, 109, 138
Vedas, 37, 77, 109, 113, 115, 122, 135
virahotkaṇṭhitā nāyikā, 75
Viṣṇu, 25, 44, 46, 61, 90, 109, 116, 122
Viṣṇudās, 4
Viṣṇusvāmin, 1, 5, 11, 78, 131, 133
Viśvāmitra, 137
Viśvanāth Jāni, 4, 10, 18

Viṭṭhala, 54, 120, 123
Viṭṭhalanātha, 18
Vraja, 37, 44, 115, 122, 124
Vrindā, 81, 82, 84, 87, 95, 99, 100
Vrindavana, 29, 32, 39, 43, 44, 45, 49, 54, 59, 61, 85, 89, 90, 92, 124
Vyāsa, 37, 115
Vyūha, 112
Yādava, 74, 109
Yadu, 27
Yadunātha, 94
Yamunā, 42, 56
Yaśodā, 29, 42, 50, 52, 100, 122
Yoga, 112
yogīs, 97, 112, 115, 120, 129
Yudhiṣṭhira, 122